AROUND

Barcelona
and Sitges

Barcelona
and Sitges

By Paul Clements

Thomas Cook
Publishing

Published by Thomas Cook Publishing
PO Box 227
The Thomas Cook Business Park
19–21 Coningsby Road
Peterborough
PE3 8XX

E-mail: books@thomascook.com

ISBN: 1841573 655

Text © 2003 Thomas Cook Publishing
Maps © 2003 Thomas Cook Publishing

Head of Publishing: Donald Greig
Project Editor: Jennifer Doherty
Editor: Jane Egginton
Proofreader: Jan Wiltshire

Design and Layout: Studio 183 Ltd
Cover Design and Artwork: Studio 183 Ltd

City maps drawn by: Studio 183 Ltd
Transport maps: Transport Cartographic Service

Scanning: Studio 183 Ltd

Printed and bound in Spain by: Artes Gráficas Elkar, Loiu, Spain

Written and researched by Paul Clements
Photography: Gavin Harrison

Additional photography:
Pictures Colour Library: page 51
Neil Setchfield: page 116
Spectrum Colour Library: page 119

Cover photographs: Gavin Harrison, except female couple shot on back cover
which belongs to Queerstock.com

Paul Clements wishes to thank Paul Joseph, for your invaluable help with the research
on this book; Donald Greig, for talking me into it in the first place; Jennifer Doherty
and Studio 183 for your professionalism in pulling this project together. It's been a blast.

Contents

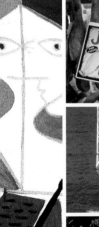

CONTENTS

My Kind of Town...

I've been in love with Barcelona since my university days when my Catalan roommate gave me an exhaustive tour of his home town. On subsequent return trips I have hung out in the city's gay bars, practising chat-up lines in broken Spanish with surprising success. In my book, that's reason enough to love a place and its people.

Travelling is not only a passion, it's my job. As deputy editor of British Airways' glossy magazine, *High Life*, I get to see the world – though Barcelona remains my favourite city by a long lead. When not sitting cross-legged in a Tokyo tofu restaurant, haring around the neighbourhoods of Santiago de Chile (another favourite city), or in New York interviewing the likes of Mariah Carey and Tom Jones in their hotel suites, I also write a monthly city guide for *Business Life*. So I get around.

I have been the guest 'travel-shooter' on BBC Radio 1's *Sunday Surgery* phone-in show and hosted the station's annual travel week webchat. I am also the author of *Out Around London*, another guidebook in this series.

Equally relevant to my credentials is that I remain the longest serving editor of *The Pink Paper*, Britain's lesbian and gay newspaper. I took up this position at the age of 21, which made me the youngest editor of a national title. After that, and despite by then being something of a professional homosexual, I was invited to join the *Mail on Sunday* to work on the entertainment and news review, *Night&Day*. My next career move will, I hope, involve relocation to Barcelona.

But until I've mastered the local languages (plural) and found that perfect apartment in the Eixample, or something in Poble Nou with a sea view, you'll find me propping up the city's bars every few months. When in Barça, mine's a *vodka limón*. Do come and say *hola*.

Barcelona shore

Out in Barcelona

Barcelona has made many names for itself since hosting the Olympic Games in 1992, a defining moment in its 2,000-year history. Today, it is known the world over as a design city, a party town, a gastro capital, and a gay magnet – the unquestionable jewel of the Mediterranean. Call it what you will, when it comes to names, names, names, Barcelona is a label queen.

What Barcelona's got, she flaunts. And you name it, she's got it. Spain's second city is cradled between the last gasp of the Pyrenees and the shores of the Mediterranean, and is blessed with sun, sea, sand and sexy people in every direction. Mere minutes from the city centre, its beaches are perfect for a cooling dip in summer (if there's space), or for an afternoon sashay in winter. And, 20 minutes down the Costa Dorada, there's the truly wonderful town of Sitges. This former fishing port is, after Ibiza, Europe's gayest beach playground. You'll find a mini guide to Sitges starting on page 99.

Finding your way in Barcelona is as easy as finding things to see and to do. The city is neatly divided into 'uptown' and 'downtown' by Plaça de Catalunya – the huge historic central square with fountains and benches where idlers come to mill and tourists come to twirl in awe as they get their bearings. Although never referred to as such, uptown is the Eixample (or 'expansion') which filthy rich Catalans, tired of being confined to the brimming gothic city, colonised in the late 19th century. They commissioned grand homes from leading architects of the movement known as Modernisme – a Catalan take on Art Nouveau and not to be confused with what is known elsewhere as Modernism. Guess which community flocked to resurrect this architecturally flamboyant district after dictator Franco allowed it to go to seed?

Most famous of all Modernista architects is Antonio Gaudí, whose creations have become landmarks of Barcelona. His most cherished and emblematic work is the Sagrada Família, an unfinished cathedral with soaring towers and fantastical façades depicting scenes from the Bible in rapturous detail.

Down from Plaça de Catalunya is the cobbled labyrinth of the Old City, whose streets date back to the 13th century. These passageways are as narrow and gnarled as they are absorbing, a world away from the Eixample, and filled with little shops and unexpected squares, bustling cafés and bars. The old quarter (Barri Gòtic), home to Barcelona's other cathedral, the romanesque masterpiece La Seu, is separated from the once seedy but now scrubbed up Raval area by the city's most famous address, La Rambla: a mile-long café-strewn avenue which literally paves the way to the Mediterranean.

At its foot is the Old Port (Port Vell). Thanks to extensive renovations completed for the Olympic Games, this is actually new, and now the largest working port in Europe. Then there are the beaches of Barceloneta, which stretch for miles along the coast, again belatedly cleaned up to provide a suitably stunning backdrop for the Olympic Village (Vila Olímpic). Mar Bella, an accessible nudist beach around 30 minutes' stroll from Barceloneta metro station, is where the gays are.

In the opposite direction from the port is Montjuïc, a craggy, 200m-high outpost that's home to the stadiums and sporting arenas which hosted the Olympic Games, as well as a bevy of museums, galleries and leafy walkways left over from the much-vaunted International Exhibition, held there in 1929.

So where should you begin? Most newcomers start with La Rambla. Indeed, it would be hard to avoid this street which has been Barcelona's backbone since it was paved and turned into a boulevard in the late 18th century. It is a feast for the senses and a suitable place to take the city's temperature – which is invariably hot, with a racing pulse.

Here, you'll also get a feel for kinks in the social fabric, which is by turns oh-so elegant and grungily bohemian. Veer off La Rambla – with its glitzy department stores at the top and seedier flavour at the other end – and head deeper into the Old City. The chances are you will either find *granja* milk bars full of well-to-do society ladies gossiping in brisk

Catalan and sipping *xocolata* (hot chocolate), or you will bump into edgy characters (beggars, drug addicts and transvestite prostitutes) seemingly in search of a Pedro Almodóvar film. That is half the attraction of Barcelona. She is a diva.

As with every diva, there is hidden sadness here. She is a city masking a painful past. Barcelona is the capital of Catalonia (Catalunya), a semi-autonomous region in the north-east of the Iberian peninsula which has for centuries been fighting to achieve independence from Madrid.

And mind your language here. Barcelona is not Spanish. In this bilingual city the mother tongue is Catalan, a thriving romance language spoken by over 7 million people (and not just inside Catalonia's borders, but in neighbouring France and Andorra, too). This language not only has much in common with Castillian Spanish, but fizzes between the teeth and sounds – say some – like a drunk Spaniard attempting French. Everywhere in Barcelona the pecking order is clear: Catalan first, Castillian second. Although both languages have equal legal status, all street signs are in Catalan, as are many menus, and tourists receive an extra warm smile if they greet shopkeepers with a tentative 'Bon dia' (Catalan for hello) instead of 'Buenos dias'. A few useful expressions are included on page 146.

But what about the gay scene? Homosexuality was decriminalised in Spain in 1822 and the age of consent was brought down to 12 years for both heterosexuals and homosexuals in 1996. Two years later, the Catalan government proved its liberal mettle by recognising gay partnerships in law. Barcelona has long been at the gay vanguard, championing Spain's first Pride event in 1977. It now alternates as host for the national gay day with Madrid, when scene mavens in both cities can be bothered to organise one. (See p.89.)

In terms of a gay village, Barcelona's is the gridded quarter in the left Eixample, north of Gran Via, between Comte d'Urgell and Aribau – and commonly referred to as the 'Gaixample' (gay-zhyam-play). A quick stroll along Consell de Cent, Diputació, Casanova and Muntaner reveals a concentration of gay bars, clubs and shops. Gay men and lesbians mix well here and both are welcome in each other's bars. There is even one men-only sleaze joint, Martins (see p.82), which has a big transgender following, especially with those with pneumatic busts. But broadly speaking the Eixample is boyztown. If the girls want to be alone they head to Gràcia, the well-heeled neighbourhood north of Avinguda Diagonal – or to Sitges or Figueres, some 100 kilometres north, where there's a burgeoning lesbian population. (See p.115.)

For all its similarities with world-class destinations like London, New York and Sydney, Barcelona is not a 24-hour city. Most shops close for three hours in the afternoon for a siesta – an old-fashioned concept these days. But you'll be grateful for the nap, as bars stay open until the last person leaves. Here, getting home as the sun comes up is considered reasonable behaviour.

Barcelona has a rhythm, which

Human statues

translates on the gay scene into a strict routine. Bars fill and empty with quartz-like precision. A night out begins comparatively late and certainly never before 11pm, when the bars are still empty. Start at Punto for drinks, then at midnight head to Dietrich or Z:eltas for a spot of dancing and mingling. Then at 3am, it's on to your club of choice. After that, there's always an after-hours club to be found (ask any cloakroom or door attendant for flyers). Similarly, if it's sauna fun that you are after, they tend to get busy during the siesta. Going out with gay friends requires synchronised watches.

People here are very interested in checking each other out, so dress to impress. Even the smallest and quietest neighbourhood bar won't just have a resident DJ but a resident drag act, too. During the course of a night expect the lights to be dimmed and a space to be cleared for an immaculately turned out female impersonator (or, in classier places, a post-op transsexual) to lip synch her way through some full-lunged power ballad.

But that's quintessential Barcelona. What can you do except applaud wildly and shout 'Viva la diva!'

Sagrada sculpture

Stepping Out

When in Barcelona, you don't need a checklist of sights. There is plenty to marvel at all around. But there is a handful of remarkable attractions – from instantly recognisable Gaudí landmarks to the unique minimalist summer pavilion hidden at the foot of Montjuïc – that will enrich your stay.

For all its treasures, Barcelona is a compact city that gives up its gems easily. Take them in aboard one of the many tour buses, or better still by simply walking around. The city is relatively flat and it pays to dive down alleyways that take your fancy. You are unlikely to wander too far from a metro station and are more likely to find a charming church, square or café to call your own.

My Top Sights

La Sagrada Família

Honeycomb spires

ⓘ Entrances on C. Sardenya and C. Mallorca 🕾 93 207 30 31 www.sagradafamilia.org
🕙 Oct–Mar daily 9am–1pm; April–Sept daily 9am–8pm 🚇 Metro: Sagrada Familia. Bus 19, 33, 34, 43, 44, 50, 51
🎟 €6; Passion tower lift €1.50

Antonio Gaudí's Sagrada Família is the most flamboyant cathedral of the modern age. Engulfing a whole block of the Eixample like a monolithic sandcastle, its dizzying honeycomb spires look like dripping wax, while its colourful sculpted façades animate the Bible story in passionate detail. It is also Barcelona's most popular attraction, pulling in more than a million slack-jawed visitors a year. Not bad for what is essentially a building site.

STEPPING OUT

The sheer scale of this visionary benchmark of modern religious architecture is breathtaking. Once the tallest building in the city, its spires reach almost 100m into the air and are coloured with ornate mosaics and decorations inspired by nature. Instead of ugly gothic gargoyles, there are doves, serpents, turtles, and even a life-size donkey. Those on either side of the nave depict the Nativity and Passion; the craggily magnificent main entrance is topped by the Glory façade. It is small wonder that Jean Cocteau called the cathedral 'a mindscraper'.

A tour should include a peek inside the newly completed nave with its tree-like stone supports, the cloister, and the vaulted chamber that will eventually support the centrepiece tower representing Christ, yet to be built. A team of international architects is now racing to finish the thing for 2026, the centenary of Gaudí's death.

Parc Güell

ⓘ C. d'Olot ⏰ 10am–dusk daily 🚇 Lesseps Buses 24, 25. Bus Turístic to the gate 🎫 Free

Parc Güell is one of Barcelona's most enchanting open spaces, a surreal wonderland of sloping terraces, fairytale pavilions and hidden recesses.

Set in forest land on a steep hill overlooking downtown, with fantastic views over the whole city, the ambitious project was completed (by Gaudí) in 1914. It features a riot of *trencadís* tiling – a decorative technique pioneered by Gaudí using broken glass and ceramic to give sculptures a hardwearing but colourful mosaic coat – and is full of the architect's characteristically fanciful features and naturalistic exuberance. There is the Sala Hipóstila, originally intended as a market hall, a grand staircase 'guarded' by a mosaic salamander, a winding ceramic bench picked out with *trencadís*.

Gaudí was keen on puzzles and

Remarkable roofs

opaque symbolism. Here you'll find a hermetically sealed chapel (no one has ever worked out how to get in), a maze-like network of rambling paths and viaducts, and the Torre Rosa, the architect's former home which is now a small, shrine-like museum, the Casa-Museu Gaudí.

Casa-Museu Gaudí

ⓘ Inside Park Güell, C. de Carmen
📞 93 284 64 46
⏰ Oct–April 10am–2pm daily; May–Sept 4pm–7pm daily 🎫 €3

Boqueria market

La Rambla

🚇 Metros: Catalunya, Liceu, Drassanes

No trip to Barcelona would be complete without a stroll along its most celebrated street. Running from Plaça de Catalunya all the way to the rejuvenated port, all roads seem to lead to this wide, leafy, part-pedestrianised avenue, which to the gay poet Lorca was the most beautiful in the world. Although much of La Rambla's 19th-century charm has worn off – until the pre-1992 clean-up it had been a particularly dangerous red-light district – it is still home to some of the city's most charming landmarks. These include the Boqueria market, the Liceu opera house and the Font de las Canaletes – a fountain from which, legend has it, every tourist must drink in order to ensure a safe return to the city. There's also a pavement mosaic by Miró and a variety of churches to be taken in.

But the greatest pleasure to be had along this kilometre-long drag is the walk itself. An artery of theatricality, La Rambla throbs with life at all times of the day and night. (See p. 29–35.)

Catedral de Barcelona (La Seu)

ℹ️ Plaça de la Seu 📞 93 315 15 54
🕐 Daily 8am–1.30pm, 4pm–7.30pm
🚇 Jaume II. Bus 17, 19, 40, 45 🆓 Free

An antidote to Barcelona's more famous cathedral (see p. 13), the gothic masterpiece of La Seu is – unlike Gaudí's half-finished effort – in full working order as the city's spiritual bedrock.

Built in 1298 on the site of a former Roman temple that was later occupied by two churches (a 4th-century baptistery destroyed by maurauding Moors and a replacement Romanesque basilica), it wasn't finished until 150 years later, in 1448 – a familiar story in Barcelona. Even then, it had to make do without a western-facing main façade overlooking Plaça Nova for another four centuries. Seeing it floodlit at night is enough to convince anyone that it was worth the wait.

The finished La Seu was finally unveiled in 1888 when finances permitted the façade's construction using plans dating back to the 15th century. Consequently, it is a mishmash of Gothic style and neo-Gothic stylings, with Baroque and Romanesque chapels, Renaissance screens and Modernista stained-glass windows. Thrillseekers will be more interested in the lift that whisks visitors to the roof for superb views across the Barri Gòtic.

But there's plenty to be seen inside. Don't miss the low-slung crypt containing the alabaster sarcophagus of Sant Eulàlia, a patroness of Barcelona whose

The old cathedral

breasts were sliced off by the Romans during one of 13 grisly torture sessions prior to her crucifixion.

Yet the most popular and fanciful part is the 14th-century cloister, with a shady, palm-fronded garden at its centre, home to a family of honking geese which has been there for five centuries. Perhaps the best time to visit is Sunday morning, when the cathedral provides an imposing backdrop for groups of mostly elderly dancers in the Plaça de la Seu performing the *sardana*, a local hotstep which is surprisingly fiendish to pull off.

Fundació Joan Miró

ℹ️ A. l'Estadi, Parc de Montjuïc
📞 93 329 19 08   www.bcn.fjmiro.es
Ⓜ️ Paral.lel (then funicular), or Espanya then up the escalators. Bus 50, 61
💶 All exhibitions €7.50, €3 concessions. Permanent collection only €4, €2 concessions

Barcelona has two world-class museums devoted to two masters of modern art: Pablo Picasso and Joan Miró, both of whom worked extensively in the city. While the

Picasso Museum contains no truly major pieces, the Fundació Joan Miró houses the most comprehensive selection of its namesake's work anywhere in the world. Take an audioguide, or a guided tour in English – or plot your own route through his colourful career (pun intended).

Housed in a splendid white building on Montjuïc, specially built in 1975 by his friend Josep Lluís Sert, the collection of more than 400 paintings and sculptures opens with a remarkable room of tapestries. After an exploration of his younger works, it's on to the real meat: the best of his Cubist and Surrealist periods. Highlights include the set of 50 lithographs completed after the Civil War, called *Barcelona Series*. On top of the building is a quiet sculpture terrace, with Miró's playful 3D works.

Of all the intriguing non-Miró pieces here, most popular is the mesmerising mercury fountain by Alexander Calder, first exhibited in 1937 alongside Picasso's *Guernica*.

Even for non-art fans, the Fundació is a great excuse to ride the funicular from Paral.lel metro (*see p.51*), and there's a decent café, too.

Fundació Joan Miró

Montjuïc

🅼 Espanya. Funicular from Paral.lel.
Bus 50 and others from Plaça d'Espanya

Montjuïc – the hilly parkland rising up beside the port – means 'Jewish mountain' in Catalan. It is known today to Barcelonans as 'pink mountain', not least because its bushes are full of gay men pretending to walk their dogs in the thicket, or around the Teatre Grec ampitheatre, regardless of the time of day or weather.

Its prime interest, however, is as a historical location for some spectacular sporting events and artistic landmarks. It was here that much of the 1992 Olympic Games were played out, in the Estadi Olímpic and the swimming lanes of the Piscines Bernat Picornell, which are open to the public (*see p. 97*). Visually, the Anella Olímpic's crowning glory

is the Torre Calatrava, a ghost-white looped mast that dominates the Plaça Sant Jordi and also doubles as a giant sundial.

Art fans will appreciate the Fundació Joan Miró (see opposite); the spectacular Museu Nacional d'Art de Catalunya inside the Palau Nacional (*see pp. 45, 48*); the recreated Pavelló Barcelona, and German architect Mies van der Rohe's marble and onyx pavilion.

Olympic pool

Parc de la Ciutadella

ℹ️ Passeig Picasso ☀️ April–Sept 8am–9pm daily; Oct–Mar 8am–8pm daily 🅼 Arc de Triom, Barceloneta. Bus 14, 39, 40, 42, 51, 100, 541 🆓 Free

What this park between La Ribera and the Vila Olímpic lacks in looks, it more than makes up for in history and folkloric attractions. Steeped in incident, it was originally a citadel torn into the heart of La Ribera by the king's troops after the 1714 siege of Barcelona so that they could train their cannons on the unruly Catalan city from within. In later, more settled years, it was converted into a 150-acre public park (and in 1888 hosted the Universal Exhibition, at which Modernisme was unveiled to the wider world).

Today, it's a busy recreational and educational park where families come for mind-broadening day trips, and the style brigade from the nearby Born district come to stretch their legs during the siesta. Its highlights include the zoo, the Museu d'Art Modern (which currently shares premises with the Catalan Parliament), and the impressive Modernista brick edifice of the Museu de Zoologia. There's also low-key cruising to be had around the Cascadas, a grandiose fountain-cum-monument.

Architectural lines

Pavelló Barcelona

ℹ️ A. Marquès de Comillas 📞 93 423 40 16 www.miesbcn.com 🕐 10am–8pm daily (6.30pm Nov–Mar) Ⓜ️ Espanya. Bus 50 🚌 €3.40

Of all the museums and attractions on Montjuïc, perhaps the most intriguing – and certainly the one with the fewest exhibits – is this sleek summer pavilion. Conceived by genius German designer Ludwig Mies van der Rohe, who made famous the mantra 'less is more', the cool one-storey construction is a landmark of rationalist architecture. It will thrill anyone who's ever drooled over a copy of *Wallpaper* magazine.

A boxy structure built from onyx, chrome and glass, with no definite purpose other than to 'enclose space' (as one of Mies van der Rohe's contemporaries swooned) and blur the boundary between outdoors and indoors, its clean lines were revolutionaries when unveiled, the Germany entry to Barcelona's 1929 International Exhibition.

There's little to see inside – this is architecture for architecture's sake after all, although the on-site shop has the trendiest general Barcelona postcards in town.

Passeig de Gràcia

Ⓜ️ Metro: Plaça de Catalunya, Passeig de Gràcia, Diagonal; Buses: 17, 24, 28, the Tom bús

Barcelona's other great avenue (after La Rambla), this broad, plane-tree-lined boulevard is famed as much today for its shopping as for its extraordinary concentration of Modernista architecture. To walk along it from Plaça de Catalunya is to pass some of the most important works of the period – mostly mansion blocks commissiond by the city's status-aware citizens in the late-19th century.

But look up above the shop fronts and you'll drop your bags in awe. Within a few blocks along this one street there's La Pedrera, a cream cake of a building (by Gaudí, naturally) with undulating windows and balconies and not a straight line in sight; Casa Battló, Gaudí's rippling dragon house, which was recently opened to visitors for the first time; and Casa Amatller, a quite different mansion house altogether, built for a chocolate magnate and looking like a gingerbread house.

The rippling dragon house

Boats at Port Vell

The beaches

🚇 Barceloneta, Ciutadella Vila Olímpica, Bogatell, Poble Nou (for Mar Bella). Buses: 36, 41

Thanks to the 1992 Olympics, Barcelona now has some of the best inner-city beaches in Europe, which are walking distance from the bottom of La Rambla. This being a city built on looks, even the concrete sunloungers at Platja Nova Icària are works of art.

The westernmost point of interest is Port Vell (Old Port), Barcelona's innermost working harbour with an imposing (but uninspiring) darkened glass shopping complex, Maremàgnum, the city's aquarium and an Imax cinema. Rather than bother with air-conditioned precincts, tread the Rambla del Mar instead, a wavy boardwalk that rotates to let boats pass, and admire pop artist Roy Lichtenstein's mosaic sculpture, *Barcelona Head*, on Moll de la Fusta. Here you can also hire a catamaran to tour the harbour. (*See p.57.*)

Heading east on foot is beachy Barceloneta. Its *platjas* stretch for several kilometres from Sant Sebastià (where you can take the precarious and expensive cable car to Montjuïc – *see p.51*), so pack a swimming costume – or head a couple of kilometres past the Port Olímpic to Mar Bella, the nudist section popular with gays. If it's water sports you're after, there's a hire centre here.

On the way is Port Olímpic, a haven for rollerbladers and gentle cyclists (for hire details – *see pp.96–97*).

Heavenly spires

Around Town

Barcelona began life as Barcino, a cramped walled Roman city – remnants of which can still be seen around the Barri Gòtic, Europe's largest medieval neighbourhood – before busting its seams intermittently to form overspill neighbourhoods. So, in the mid-1700s Barceloneta was built on reclaimed land around the harbour. The Eixample sprang up on former farmland in 1854, after Madrid conceded that the Bourbon walls causing chronic overcrowding in La Ribera could be torn down. Montjuïc was landscaped in 1914 to provide green space and a lofty platform to house the city's art collections, museums and (latterly) its conference halls. Most recently, in the mid-1980s came the transformation of the grotty industrial port into a waterside playground. Consequently, Barcelona has been bequeathed a handful of distinct quarters, each a specific time capsule of history and architecture, with its own look and feel, and each detailed in the coming chapters.

The Eixample

Split in to a left (Esquerra de l'Eixample) and a right (Dreta de l'Eixample) quarter, which divide along a former tram line at C. de Balmes, the Eixample was colonised by Gaudí and lesser-known (though no less important) contemporaries like Lluís Domènech i Montaner and Puig i Cadafalch. While the area's biggest tourist draw remains the Sagrada Família and the shops along the Passeig de Gràcia (many of which occupy stunning Modernista landmarks), the streets themselves are a fantastical wonderland of grandiose set pieces. These include Casa Amatller, splashed with pink and burgundy ceramics; Casa Milà (the cream cake-like La Pedrera); Casa de les Puntxes (or House of Spikes); and the world's only UNESCO-protected hospital, Santa Creu i Sant Pau by Domènech i Montaner. Even the humblest corner pharmacies from the period retain their ornate shop signs with stylistic flourishes, and the stone street benches

which support magnificent wrought-iron lampposts betray lusty Modernista stylings.

Of the two, the Left Eixample is the poorer relation – it has its share of visual frippery but less by way of must-see attractions – but it happens to be where gay life came to flourish, post-Franco. Now home to the city's village, it has earned the nickname of the Gaixample. *(See p.25.)*

A DAY OUT

Given the size of the Eixample, which stretches from C. Tarragona and Sants train station to C. Independència and the decidedly unlovely Plaça Glòries Catalanes roundabout, it's advisable to set aside the best part of a day to see its major sights. That said – and despite the quarter's gentle uphill incline (when facing away from the sea) – it is eminently walkable.

Our walking tour starts in Plaça de Catalunya at the foot of Passeig de Gràcia, Eixample's swanky shopping belt. This is home to some of the most noteworthy Modernista landmarks the city has to offer, with dazzling creations paving every step of the way. The first major point of interest is the block known as the Mansana de la Discòrdia. Between C. Consell de Cent (Barcelona's answer to London's Old Compton Street) and C. d'Aragó is the 'block of discord', so called because each *casa* was built to outshine the next in sheer ostentation. First up is Casa Lleó Morera, a once spectacular residential block by Domènech i Montaner, which was later ruined at street level by a shop-front conversion. At No. 41 is Casa Amatller, Josep Puig i Cadafalch's ceramic-stippled fairytale hideaway, topped off by a stepped pyramid façade. Entry is restricted to the lobby and the first floor but here you can get further information about the movement and its landmarks, as well as free guided tours of the Mansana de la Discòrdia, from the Centre del Modernisme housed here.

The most impressive sight along the Mansana de la Discòrdia (though, legend has it, the beholder has to decide) is Gaudí's offering, Casa Battló, a so-so townhouse he set about refurbishing with extraordinary panache and vision, dressing it up with dragon imagery. The secrets of the equally sublime apartments and roof terrace were finally opened to visitors in 2002.

Round the corner on C. d'Aragó is the Fundació Antoni Tàpies, a modern art gallery. A prototype red-brick Modernista building, its roof is decorated with a mad looping wire sculpture that's particularly remarkable when lit up at night.

Further up the Passeig on the right-hand side is Casa Milà, better known as La Pedrera, a honey-white show-stopping cornerpiece apartment block by Gaudí. Its stonework is sculpted so that its windows look like mini-caves, with contrasting black ironwork (another Gaudí speciality) forming balconies cast like fishing nets. The insides are also a must-see.

Then it's around the corner, turning right onto C. del Rosselló –
stopping briefly to take in the gothic palace, Museu de Mùsica – to the
maddest house on A. Diagonal: the Casa de les Puntxes, or House of
Spikes, a pointy steepled neo-Gothic nightmare. Shiver, then keep
walking along Diagonal, turning left down C. de Mallorca. Sanctuary is in
the looming form of the Sagrada Família.

Set aside plenty of time to pay homage, to marvel at its size and
unworldly beauty, and to queue for the lift to the top of the spires. When
you are done, the best vantage point for photographs is from the A. de
Gaudí. This also has the best cafés in which to cool your heels before the
next bedazzling landmark, handily perched at the top of this avenue: the
Hospital de la Santa Creu i Sant Pau, by Domènech i Montaner.

With its monolithic brick pavilions set in sprawling grounds, this is a
Modernista head-spinner, a working hospital whose intricate tiled
buildings are architectural aromatherapy, calming to the very soul.
Designated a World Heritage Site, it's a magnificent mini-city worth an
hour of idling time.

If you've got the stamina or the inclination, it's a 20-minute walk
downhill from here along C. dels Dos de Maig to Els Encants, an
unprepossessing flea market selling all sorts of junk and secondhand
treasure. Bear in mind that the best bargains are to be had in the early
morning (it opens at 8am), and do your Eixample tour accordingly – in
reverse, if scouring's more your thing than sightseeing.

La Pedrera

Out to Lunch

You're never going to go hungry in the Eixample. The Passeig de Gràcia is lined with Basque tapas chains (like **Tapa Tapa, Ba Ba Ree Ba, Qu Qu, Txapela**) and British-style sandwich bars like **Fresh & Ready. Café Torino** (*see p. 76*) is a popular and pricey crowd-watching spot for a coffee and a bite.

Alternatively, the **El Fornet d'en Rossend** chain dotted around the Eixample offers a Med interpretation of a British tea room, with a series of slightly sterile drawing room salons, and newspapers on rollers. Great for a quick restorative *pa amb tomàquet* (baguette rubbed with tomato), cake or muffin.

For a square meal, the best deal is at **Castro** (*see pp. 69–70*) in the Gaixample. The gay-run restaurant, thoughtfully decorated with chains and handcuffs, offers a varied and reasonably priced set lunch menu. The style set also frequent **Tenorio** (*see p. 75*), an international brasserie with a velvet-rope enclave of outdoor tables.

For something cheap and cheerful, make up your own mezze plate at gay coffee bar **Daphnes** (*see p. 87*), which is all snakeskin bar stools and hippy-dippy purple décor. Low-key and never busy, the staff are always helpful.

Around the Sagrada Família, ignore the touristy snack bars in the immediate surrounding area and head instead for **Babilonia** on Av. de Gaudí. You get a perfect view of the cathedral from the terrace tables as you wait for your plate of steaming pasta to arrive.

Daphnes

THE GAIXAMPLE

Barcelona's gay village is relatively compact, occupying a couple of blocks of the left-hand Eixample – and known colloquially as the Gaixample. The streets around C. Consell de Cent and C. Muntaner are peppered with gay bars, restaurants, shops, saunas and the occasional gay *hostal*. However, except for the odd rainbow flag, you'd never know it by walking around by day – these streets are residential and only take on a pink hue after hours.

FOLLOWING GAUDÍ'S EIXAMPLE

If there's one man who can be said to have built Barcelona as many picture it in their mind's eye, it is Antonio Gaudí, the Modernista architect whose creamily spired Sagrada Família cathedral is the city's emblematic landmark. Though the Modernisme style was championed by many Catalan architects, Gaudí's influence is keenest felt in the city, nowhere more starkly than in the Eixample (pronounced Eh-zham-play), the 19th-century quarter which contains most of his important private commissions.

OUTLINES

Dramatic detail

CASA AMATLLER / CENTRE DEL MODERNISME

ℹ️ Passeig de Gràcia 41
📞 93 488 01 39
www.bcn.es
🕐 Mon–Sat 10am–7pm
Ⓜ️ Passeig de Gràcia.
Bus: 7, 16, 17, 22, 24, 28
💳 Free

Modernista architect Puig i Cadafalch's Gothic contribution to the block of houses known as Mansana de la Discòrdia, commissioned by competing bourgeois families in clashing styles. Inside, there's an information centre selling books of discount coupons to major Modernista landmarks like the Sagrada Família and La Pedrera.

CASA BATTLÓ

ℹ️ Passeig de Gràcia 43
📞 93 216 03 06
www.casabatllo.es
🕐 Daily 9am–2pm
Ⓜ️ Passeig de Gràcia.
Bus: 7, 16, 17, 22, 24, 28
💳 €10

Gaudí at his most emblematic. Since the dragon-like building was opened up to visitors for the recent 150th anniversary of his birth, the public can now not only enjoy the shimmering exterior, but also the subterranean, Captain Nemo-esque hallway, fish-scale walls, a succession of increasingly grand wood-panelled drawing rooms in the Modernista style, plus the lavish, multi-coloured reliefs in the courtyard.

FUNDACIÓ ANTONI TÀPIES

ℹ️ C. Aragó 255
📞 93 487 03 15
fatmb@server.ibernet.com
🕐 Tues–Sun 10am–8pm
Ⓜ️ Passeig de Gràcia.
Bus: 7, 16, 17, 22, 24, 28
💳 €4.50

A former printworks and an early Modernista work by Domènech i Montaner in bare brick and iron. It now houses a curious collection of contemporary Catalan and non-Western art – as well as the 'greatest hits' of Miró's contemporary, Antoni Tàpies: a table pinned to the wall, a wardrobe of clothes, more clothes but daubed with paint and draped over a chair. You get the idea. If anguished modern art is not your thing, content yourself with the exterior – the roof sculpture, a jungle of iron loops, is particularly stunning at night.

CASA MILÁ/LA PEDRERA

ℹ️ 92 Passeig de Gràcia, 261 C. de Provença
📞 93 484 59 95
www.funcaixacat.com
🕐 Daily 10am–8pm
Ⓜ️ Diagonal. Bus: 7, 16, 17, 22, 24, 28
💳 €6

Marvel at Gaudí's undulating stone exterior, then see his genius at work inside. The courtyards, loft and rooftop (which is tiled using hundreds of broken Cava bottles) are all open to the public, as is one of the apartments (El Pis de la Pedrera), furnished in the Modernista style. Entry to the temporary exhibitions is free, accessible via the fantastic stairwell. In summer (July to September), the roof terrace becomes a vibey bar. Book a table in advance and expect to pay about €10 for the stupendous views.

Fundació Antoni Tàpies

CASA DE LES PUNTXES

ℹ️ A. Diagonal 416–420

✖️ Closed to the public

Ⓜ️ Verdaguer. Buses: 20, 39, 45, 47

It's not the mock-medieval castle-like façade that's the pull here (accomplished in pretty brickwork though it is), but the turrets topped off with syringe-like needles from which Puig i Cadafalch's Casa Terrades gets its 'House of Spikes' nickname. Irregular in shape and decidedly untheatrical, de les Puntxes is a stark contrast to the more flamboyant, playful

examples of Modern-ista architecture.

LA SAGRADA FAMÍLIA
See pp.13–14.

HOSPITAL DE SANT PAU

ℹ️ C. Sant Antoni María Claret 167

☎️ 93 291 90 00

🕐 Open daily

Ⓜ️ Hospital de Sant Pau. Bus: 15, 19, 20, 35, 45, 47, 50, 51, 92

Not only a prime example of Modern-isme in all its bricked glory, but a working hospital with no two wards the same. The entrance hall is stippled with gorgeous

pink ceramics, and you'll need to set aside at least half an hour to wander the solemn gardens, the cobbled streets and subterr-anean accessways.

ELS ENCANTS

ℹ️ Plaça de les Glòries Catalanes

🕐 Mon, Wed, Fri, Sat, 8am–2pm

Ⓜ️ Glòries. Bus 7, 56

A buzzy flea market in one of the Eixample's most unprepossessing corners. Go early to rummage among the stock, or stand back and watch local characters socialising.

Fountain of delight

La Rambla

Barcelona's most famous street is its magnificent mile-long café and tree-lined artery cutting through the heart of the Old City (Ciutat Vella), from Plaça de Catalunya to the sea. But in the 14th century, long before it became a fashionable boulevard on which to promenade (or *ramblejeant* in Catalan), it was a covered sewer. The stink lingered on, especially noticeable during the dark years of Franco's reign. Then it was more a magnet for hookers, touts and pickpockets – and elements of all three remain today.

To the east of La Rambla is the Barri Gòtic, a maze of medieval streets whose sights are worth a day's exploration in their own right. (*See pp.37–43.*) This chapter, then, will take you for a walk along that city's celebrated address, with diversions into the once-seedy former merchant district of El Raval to its west, now an up-and-coming arty quarter. When strolling the Rambla, the trick is to take your time. There's no need to rush, you're on Barcelona time. The chances are the crowds won't let you move off at your usual walking pace anyway...

A DAY OUT

Most visitors to the Rambla (that is, those not staying in its numerous budget hotels and hostels) pour out of Catalunya metro, the landmark fountain-strewn square linking the old town with the new. Along the Rambla de les Canaletes – the first of five seamlessly connected strips that make up the Rambla – the human traffic is heaviest. Tourists gather at the Font de les Canaletes, a fountain from which all visitors are invited to drink in order to ensure their safe return to the city.

Next is the Rambla dels Estudis, where the general hustle and bustle is given a new soundtrack provided by the twitter of caged birds, hence its nickname La Rambla dels Ocells. If the sight of scrawny parrots and strung-up chickens on sale at the market stalls here is upsetting, nip down C Bonsuccés – a favourite for second-hand vinyl and world music junkies – into the Raval district. You can easily lose the crowds by slipping into its sleek museum, Museu d'Art Contemporani de Barcelona (MACBA). On this side of the Rambla, there are also many fine newish *plaças* (squares) to discover.

Back on the main drag, where La Rambla dels Estudis becomes La Rambla de Sant Josep (better known as La Rambla de las Flores, thanks to its abundance of flower stalls), is the Església de Betlem, a 17th-century remnant built when the boulevard was lined with churches rather than cafés. Its sorry appearance today belies its recent past; it was looted and burned out during the Civil War. For those with an interest in

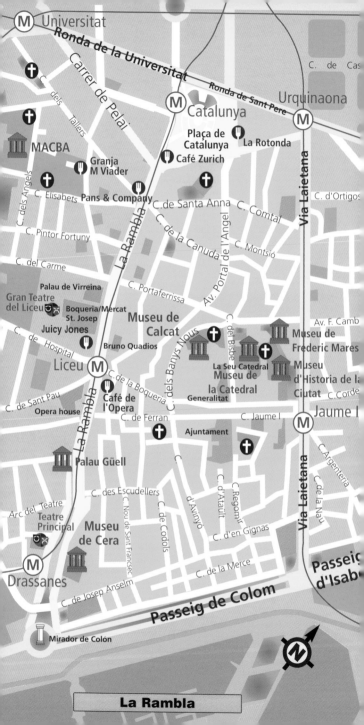

La Rambla

contemporary art, the nearby converted Palau de Virreina is an increasingly popular stop-off, thanks to a hip new curator.

If you're missing the roar of the crowds, carry on to the Mercat de Sant Josep, the lively, iron-framed food market known as La Boqueria, which is a feast for all the senses. Go shopping for the freshest fruit and veg, as well as every foodstuff imaginable, from sticky sweets like *turrón* (a brittle, nutty nougat) to whole suckling pigs, which hang from the deco fixtures. The small traders' bars dotted around the edge are good, authentic places to have a counter-top breakfast.

The halfway point of the Rambla is marked by a colourful street mosaic by Joan Miró, but don't forget to look up, too. Here, the experimental Bruno Quadros Building is decorated with Chinese dragons and parasols (now a bank, it used to be an umbrella shop). Over the road is the Escribà patisserie, housed in an exquisite Modernist *casa* with blue mosaic glittering around the door. Pop in and marvel at the cakes on display, or have a restorative coffee out back. (*See p.61.*) Then head down C. Hospital and find some peace on the Rambla de Raval, a promenade fit for the 21st century: all smooth white concrete, shady palms, and empty except for skateboarders.

Back on the Rambla proper, by the Liceu metro station, begins the lower half, which is a more restrained affair, with fewer swarming crowds. The landmark on Rambla dels Caputxins, the longest of all the Ramblas, is the Gran Teatre del Liceu opera house, rebuilt in 1999 according to original designs after it was razed by a fire. Ask in the foyer for a tour of the splendid auditorium; unless you've booked in advance, it's unlikely you'll get a seat for that night's performance.

For those who can't wait for the Barri Gòtic tour (*see pp.37–43*), now's a good time to nip through the nearby arched entrance into Plaça Reial, an arcaded but disappointingly unseemly café-edged square full of tourists, tramps and card sharks, but whose centrepiece is the Font de les Tres Gràcies, Gaudí's first civic commission.

Then head for the Palau Güell, an early Modernista by Gaudí, tucked along Carrer Nou de la Rambla. It is remarkable not only because it is one of his few major buildings outside the Eixample, but because in its mix of medieval and Moorish styles, Gaudí explored what would become his trademark use of decoration inspired by nature, such as columns of brick shaped like palm trees.

Next along is La Rambla de Santa Mónica, which retains its red-light reputation.

Before we reach the end of the Rambla, get your cameras ready for the wooden Teatre Principal, Barcelona's first theatre, built in the 16th century. Then it's on to the Mirador de Colón (across the busy Passeig de Colom), a 19th-century column topped by a statue of Christopher Columbus, inexplicably pointing not to a new world he discovered, but Italy. From the viewing platform at the top, accessible by a rickety and tiny lift, there are great views across the Mediterranean, especially if you don't have the stomach for those from the Montjuïc cable car. (*See p.51.*)

Out to Lunch

The Rambla isn't blessed with many exciting lunch options, with most places more interested in convenience than quality. The **Pans & Company** sandwich chain, of which there are a number on the Rambla, offer hot-filled *bocadillos* (baguettes) and good-value meal deals.

But the best lunch option is the psychedelic vegetarian outpost **Juicy Jones**, which offers a tasty and varied three-course *menú del dia*. This is usually a soup of the day, plus a mix of healthy salads, spicy dips and a rice course, finished off with a slice of chocolate cake – all for just €7.

If you're just after a *tallat* and *crescent* (espresso and croissant) to tide you over, you will be spoilt for choice. Try the standing-only coffee bar, **Viena**, popular with local businesspeople by day. The gay place to be (though you'd not know it until the evening) is **Café de L'Opera**, which has a beautiful roof and painted mirrors covered with Deco figurines. The bar seats are often propped up by quiet newspaper reading types and loud queens. The shine is rather taken off by the fruit machine.

One of the busiest meeting points in town, inexplicably to some, is **Café Zurich**, at the top of La Rambla, where accordionists stalk the terrace tables populated by Dutch sailors and British football fans. But there's always the self-service **La Rotonda**, on top of El Corte Inglés, notable if only for its ringside views across the city.

Fancy something distinctly Catalan? Have a pastry and *xocolata* (hot chocolate) in the late afternoon at a *granja* milk bar. One of the most celebrated is the **Granja M Viader** in the Raval. Don't worry if your Catalan isn't up to ordering – simply point to something on the drinks menu: it'll be hot, sweet and slip down a treat.

PANS & COMPANY

ℹ️ Rambla 84 and 123
☎️ 93 317 54 33 / 93 301 66 21 🚇 Liceu

JUICY JONES

ℹ️ C. Cardenal Casañas 7
☎️ 93 302 43 30
🕐 Daily 1pm–midnight
🚇 Liceu

CAFÉ VIENA

ℹ️ La Rambla 115
🚇 Liceu ☎️ 93 349 98 00

CAFÉ DE L'OPERA

ℹ️ La Rambla 74 ☎️ 93 317 75 85 🕐 Mon–Thur 8am– 2.15pm; Fri–Sat 8am–3am 🚇 Liceu

CAFÉ ZURICH

ℹ️ Plaça de Catalunya 1
☎️ 93 317 91 53 🕐 June–end Oct, Mon–Fri 8am–1am, Sat-Sun 10am–1am; End Oct–May Mon–Fri, Sun 8am–11pm, Sat 8am–midnight 🚇 Catalunya

LA ROTONDA

ℹ️ 9th floor, El Corte Inglés, Plaça de Catalunya.
(See pp.59–60.)

GRANJA M VIADER

ℹ️ 4 C. d'En Xucla
🕐 Mon 5pm–8.45pm, Tues–Sat 9am–1.45pm, 5pm–8.45pm 🚇 Liceu, Catalunya

OUTLINES

MUSEU D'ART CONTEMPORANI DE BARCELONA (MACBA)

ℹ️ Plaça dels Àngels 1
🌀 93 412 08 10
www.macba.es
☀️ Late Sept–late June,
Mon–Fri 11am–7.30pm, Sat
10am–8pm, Sun
10am–3pm; late June–late
Sept, Mon–Fri 11am–8pm,
Sat 10am–8pm, Sun
10am–3pm 🚇 Catalunya
🎟️ €5

Houses a collection of important works from Catalan artists of the latter half of the 20th century. Unlike most of Barcelona's museums, this one opens on Mondays (though not Tuesdays).

PALAU DE VIRREINA

ℹ️ La Rambla 99
🌀 93 301 77 75
☀️ Tues–Sat
11am–8.30pm, Sun
11am–3pm
🚇 Liceu 🎟️ Free

This 18th-century palace, the former home of a Peruvian diplomat, now houses an inventive photography, music and graphics museum. Its most impressive display is of the centuries-old giant dolls used in the city's street carnival dating back to 1320.

MERCAT DE SANT JOSEP (LA BOQUERIA)

See p.31.

BRUNO QUADROS BUILDING

ℹ️ La Rambla, 82 (corner
C. Cardenal Casañas)
🚇 Liceu

The sober façade of this corner mansion house was remodelled into something decidedly more prankster-like in the late 19th century. The

La Rambla

experimental motifs, such as the dragon streetlamp and decorative umbrella poked into the stonework, keep the tourists snap-happy.

GRAN TEATRE DEL LICEU

🛈 La Rambla 51–59
📞 93 485 99 00
Ⓜ Liceu
www.liceubarcelona.com/eng

Barcelona's sumptuous 19th-century opera house rose from its ashes in 1999 (not for the first time), after a meticulous reconstruction

restored its façade and interior, such is its emblematic symbolic value to the city. On a performance night, the Rambla is snarled up with Catalan ladies in their furs and fineries, and their dicky-bowed husbands. Ask at reception about the occasional guided tours of the auditorium.

PALAU GÜELL

🛈 C. Nou de la Rambla 3–5 📞 93 317 39 74
🕐 Guided tours only, Mar–Oct Mon–Sat 10am–8pm; Nov–Feb

Mon–Sat 10am–6pm
Ⓜ Liceu Ⓥ €2.40

Built as a residence for Gaudí's rich patron, the mock medieval mansion has plenty of modern design elements to thrill: elegant wood floors, funnel-shaped brickwork in the shape of palm trees, and a magnificent rooftop. There's also a tunnel that connects in to the hotel over the road (sadly closed to the public). One of Gaudí's earliest major works, it is a very popular attraction

Large landmark – the Mirador de Colón

(admission is by guided tour only) and day tickets are strictly rationed; best arrive before 11am to ensure you get in. In any case, it's worth checking out the wrought-iron gates, which are spectacular in their workmanship and almost mystic asymmetricality.

TEATRE PRINCIPAL

ⓘ La Rambla 27
📞 93 301 47 50
Ⓜ Drassanes

Barcelona's earliest surviving theatre, notable for its curved three-part façade decorated with the busts of famous actors.

MIRADOR DE COLÓN

ⓘ Plaça Portal de la Pau
📞 93 302 52 24
🕐 June–late Sept, daily 9am–8.30pm; late Sept–Mar Mon–Fri 10am–1.30pm, 3.30pm–6.30pm; Sat–Sun 10am–6.30pm; April–May Mon–Fri 10am–1.30pm, 3.30pm–7.30pm; Sat–Sun 10am–7.30pm
Ⓜ Drassanes
💲 €1.80

The world's largest shrine to Christopher Columbus was built to commemorate the discovery of the Americas. The statue at its top is made from melted-down cannons taken from the castle on Montjuïc. Though it's often shrouded by scaffolding, most visitors are content to cram into the four-man lift, which whizzes to the viewing platform, for fantastic bird's-eye panoramas across the sea and the city.

Don't mistake this crapper for a souvenir

The Catalan Crapper

It's the ultimate tacky Barcelona souvenir: a clay figurine of a cute little fella answering the call of nature, squatting with his trousers round his ankles. Say hello to the Catalan Crapper. Souvenir shops along La Rambla and around the La Seu cathedral (*see p.15*) delight tourists with *El Caganer*, who's usually dressed in a floppy felt hat and sucking on a Sherlock Holmes pipe, but is variously dolled up as priests, nuns, firemen, or even kitted out in the red and blue strip of FC Barça. At Christmas, even church nativities in Barcelona include a crapper in the congregation worshipping the virgin birth. Don't ask why, it's a Catalan thing… and you know someone back home who'll want one.

Stroll to the Museu Picasso

The Old City

Until the end of the 19th century, the Ciutat Vella, or Old City, was the heart of Barcelona, its citizens penned in by stone walls built by the Romans, who founded 'Barcino' 2,000 years ago. The maze of streets that sprang up within this confine over the centuries kept to the tight map left by the settlers, so today, the Old City is one of the best preserved medieval centres in Europe. It serves both as a reminder of Barcelona's Roman heritage and offers a window to its 'golden years' between the 12th and 15th centuries, when it became a thriving trading post and home to Catalonia's all-powerful courtly kings.

The Old City is roughly hewn into a series of neighbourhoods, each with their own distinct flavour and antiquities, with the 13th-century La Seu cathedral at its Gothic heart. Most appealing are the Barri Gòtic, the largely freeze-framed medieval hub where sections of that Roman wall, eventually torn down in the 19th century, can still be seen; La Ribera, or waterfront, that was home to Barcelona's merchant city; and El Born, the tiny cobbled quarter that has been 'reborn' in recent years after an influx of unusual boutiques and galleries. The Old City is more than a maze of scrubbed-up medieval alleyways. It's always throbbing with life, by day packed out with trendy shoppers spilling out from the stylish boutiques along C. Avinyó, then a noisy magnet for barflies on the starting blocks for an all-night party.

This walk will take in the Old City neighbourhoods enclosed by La Rambla to the left and Via Laietana to the right. For El Raval, the largest and westernmost Old City neighbourhood, see Around Town: La Rambla (*p.29*).

A DAY OUT

You don't so much need a map as a time machine to keep track of where you are in the Old City. Here, every street shows its age and the part it played in the evolution of BC Barcino into style capital BCN. One of the city's greatest pleasures is getting caught up in the Barri Gòtic's tight web of narrow alleyways. You are advised, then, to improvise your own route based on this walk.

Let's start at the top of the Old City and work around anticlockwise. Hop off the metro at Catalunya and head along the wide high-street shopping avenue Portal de l'Àngel, looking out for C Montsió, a small side street that's home to one of the most historic cafés, Els Quatre Gats (The Four Cats). Once you've had your first coffee of the day, it's over Via

The Old City

Urgell Ⓜ

Gran Via de les Corts Catalanes

Universitat Ⓜ

Universitat Ⓜ

C. d'Aribau

C.

C.

C. dels Tallers

Carrer de Pelai

Pla
Cat

C. de Sant

C. de la Ca

C. Sepúveda

C. Torres i Amat

C. de Flodidablanca

Ronda de Antoni

C. Valldonzella

Carrer del Comte d'Urgell

C. Nou de la Rambla

C. de la Riera Alta

C. del Peu de la Creu

Museu d'Art Contemporani

C. Ferlandina

C. dels Àngels

C. Elisabets

C. Pintor Fortuny

La Rambla

🍴 Bagel shop

C. Portaferrissa

Museu de Calçat

C. de Tamarit

Sant Antoni Ⓜ

C. de Sant Antoni Abat

C. de Parlament

C. de la Cera

C. del Carme

C. de Hospital

Liceu Ⓜ

C. de la Boqueria

dels Banys Nous

la Gene

V

C. de les Carretes

C. de les

C. de l'Aurora

C. de la Cadena

C. de Rieretal

Sant Pau

C. de Ferran

Ajun

Ronda de Sant Pau

Avinguda del

Paral·lel Ⓜ

C. de Vila

C. Santa Madrona

C. del

C. Nou

C. de Marques de

C. la Unió

Rambla

Palau Güell

Plaça Reial

C. des Escudellers

C. Nou de Sant Francesc

C. de Codols

d'Avinu

Paral·lel

Av. de les Drassanes

de

la

Arc del Teatre

Museu de Cera

Esglesia de la Mercé

Drassanes Ⓜ

C. de Palaudaries

C. Carrera

Museu Marítim Drassanes

Mirador de Colón

C. de Josep Anselm

Passeig

Carner

Ocean

Passeig de Josep

Moll de Barcelona

Ronda del Litoral

Moll del Poniente

🧭 N

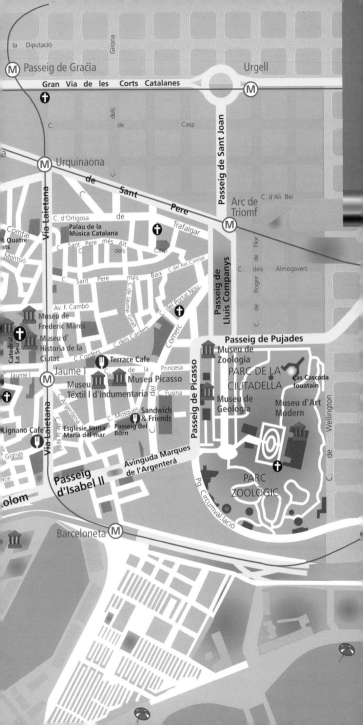

Laietana and into La Ribera for a quick tour of the Palau de la Música Catalunya, a highly decorated Modernista music hall.

Dazzled by the Palau, set off down Via Laietana, and hang a right along C. Dr Joaquim Pou. This brings you to the Catedral de Barcelona, also regarded by some as the city's finest cathedral not by Gaudí, which was built in the 13th century (though it has a

Gothic lamppost

Modernista stained-glass window by a Gaudí contemporary).

Now a cobbled junction, this is the high watermark of internecine Catalan politics. Here you'll find the Palau de la Generalitat, home of the regional government, and the Ajuntament, or City Hall, directly opposite.

A few doors away on C. Ferran, at number 42, is a plaque marking the birthplace of Catalonia's most revered artist of the 20th century, Joan Miró. For another such landmark, keep heading towards La Rambla to Plaça Reial, a café-lined square whose ornate wrought-iron lampposts were designed by the young Antonio Gaudí. If art's not your thing, nip along C. Avinyó instead for a spot of credit-card crunching in the designer boutiques.

At the foot of C. Avinyó is the towering Església de la Mercè, topped off by a statue of the Virgin that appears to float. It's worth comparing with the Església de Santa Maria del Mar, the best preserved church in gloomy Catalan Gothic style, a five-minute walk away in La Ribera on the other side of Via Laietana. Mind the traffic that hares along it.

Because of its proximity to the port, La Ribera was once the working hub of the city, and its mercantile history is now reflected in its street names, which reference tanners, wool combers, grain traders, and even semolina-makers. Today, it's home to a cluster of great museums, including the self-explanatory Museu Picasso and the Museu Tèxtil i d'Indumentària, which explores Catalan fashion though the ages, as well as the importance of its textile industry.

Keep heading along C. Montcada to check out the newly restored Mercat Santa Caterina, Barcelona's oldest market, then double back on yourself to spend the rest of the afternoon shopping in El Born.

Prized in fashion magazines the world over for its street style, the cobbled and Gothic-pillared Passatge del Born and its side streets buzz with chat, the clacking of heels and the pop-pop of scooters. Don't miss the inspiring curving lamppost-like memorial sculpture, topped with flame, in Plaça del Fosser de les Morreres, dedicated to those who died defending Barcelona during the 18th-century Spanish siege; or Plaça del Duc de Medicaneli, where Pedro Almodóvar shot his Oscar-winning *Todo Sobre Mi Madre* (*All About My Mother*).

Out to Lunch

Lunch is served

For a quick heel-cooler, try the **Lignano Café**, which besides the usual mochas and americanos has cream-topped hot chocolates, speciality teas from around the world, and a star-studded coffee menu (Café Sofia Loren comes laced with anis and grappa). A sedate spot mid-morning, it fills at lunch time with stock marketeers and local bankers, hungry for the filled sandwiches and cakes.

The most filling brunch in town can be had at slightly boho **Bagel Shop**. Alternatively, there are plenty of bleeding-edge cafés in El Born. Try **Sandwiches + Friends**, a relaxed restaurant-café with a popular outdoor terrace that's great for spotting style-setters.

For a full meal, try **Vildsvin**, a modern *taverna* serving up taste-clashes from all over Europe. Pick and mix your own lunch menu: will it be Viking fish soup followed by Bologna sausages and a Bavarian pastry ring, or Flemish broth followed by Galician hamburgers? If you can't decide, there is a *menú del dia* (prix fixe) with a beer for €5.90. The best vegetarian deals can be had at the Museu Tèxtil's cool brick courtyard café.

LIGNANO CAFÉ
- Via Laietana 3
- No phone
- Jaume

THE BAGEL SHOP
- C. Canuda 25
- 93 302 41 61
- Catalunya

SANDWICHES + FRIENDS
- Passeig del Born 27
- 93 310 07 86
- Jaume I

VILDSVIN L'ANTIGA TAVERNA
- C. Ferran 38
- 93 317 94 07
- Liceu

TERRACE CAFÉ
- Museu Tèxtil, C. Montcada 12
- 93 268 25 98
- Jaume I

Terrace lunch

OUTLINES

ELS QUATRE GATS

ⓘ C. Montsió 3

☎ 93 302 41 40

☼ Mon–Sat 9am–2am, Sun 5pm–2am Ⓜ Catalunya

This is where the local bohemian intelligentsia – including Picasso, who designed the menu front – came to sup and exchange revolutionary ideas in *fin-de-siècle* Barcelona. A landmark in its own right, it is notable for being Puig i Cadafalch's first Modernista building.

PALAU DE LA MÚSICA CATALUNYA

ⓘ C. Sant Francesc de Paula 2 ☎ 93 295 72 00

www.palaumusica.org

☼ Guided tours: 10am–3.30pm daily

Ⓜ Urquinaona ⓥ €5

See p.92.

CATEDRAL DE BARCELONA (LA SEU)

See p.15.

MUSEU D'HISTÒRIA DE LA CIUTAT

ⓘ Plaça del Rei

☎ 93 315 11 11

www.bcn.es/cultura

☼ Oct–end May Tues–Sat 10am–2pm, 4pm–8pm, Sun and hols 10am–2pm; June–end Sept Tues–Sat 10am–8pm, Sun and hols 10am–2pm Ⓜ Jaume I

For an idea of what Roman Barcino would have been like for its inhabitants, take the glass lift beneath the streets for a lively 'virtual' tour of the Roman remains under Plaça del Rei. Includes a reconstruction of how Barcelona looked at the height of its standing in the 15th century.

PALAU DE LA GENERALITAT

ⓘ Plaça de Sant Jaume

☎ 93 402 46 00

☼ www.gencat.es

Guided tours 2nd and 4th Sun only, 10.30am–1.30pm

Ⓜ Jaume 1 ⓥ Free

Home of Catalonia's parliament and its president, who has quarters in this sumptuous 15th-century palace, which also incorporates lively elements of Catalan Gothic. Access is by guided tour only, but worth the queues just to walk around the orange garden.

AJUNTAMENT DE BARCELONA

ⓘ Plaça de Sant Jaume

☎ 93 402 70 00

www.bcn.es ☼ Sun 10am–2pm Ⓜ Jaume I

ⓥ Free

Barcelona's City Hall was built in the 15th century, at the height of

its golden years, though the neo-classical façade was added when the square was opened to the public in the 19th century. Tours take you round the corridors of council power – but it's a surprisingly diverting trawl of architectural styles and flamboyant furnishings. Livelier still is the square in front, which hosts *sardana* dancing displays on Sundays.

ESGLÉSIA DE LA MERCÈ

ⓘ A. de Sarajevo 6–8

☎ 93 370 14 13

Ⓜ Dressanes

Set back from La Ribera's waterfront and a towering presence casting shadows over the Plaça de la Mercè, this Baroque church contains a Gothic statue of Our Lady of Mercy, the Virgin after whom it is named, and a font dedicated to Neptune, showing its links with all things naval. The *plaça* also hosts the ebullient Festival de la Mercè every September.

ESGLÉSIA DE SANTA MARIA DEL MAR

ⓘ Plaça de Santa Maria

☎ 93 310 23 90 Concert information 93 319 05 16

☼ Mon–Sat 9am–1:30pm, 4:30pm–8pm; Sun

9am–2pm, 5pm–8:30pm
Jaume 1 Free

With its looming oct-
agonal towers, this grey
stone 14th-century
church pushed Gothic
archictecture to its limit
– the supporting
columns span widths
greater than any other
medieval building in
the world. Gutted by a
fire in the 1800s, its
slightly glum air only
adds to the hair-shirted
majesty. Look out for
concerts held here.

MUSEU PICASSO
C. Montcada 15–23
Liceu, Arc de Triomf 93
319 63 10 Jaume I

www.museupicasso.bcn.es
Tues–Sat 10am–8pm;
Sun 10am–3pm €4.80,
free first Sunday of the
month

Contains important
works from his early
life as a painter, but is
far sketchier on his
Cubism. Blink and
you'll miss the Blue
and Pink Periods
entirely. Good selection
of ceramics and
engravings, though.

MUSEU TÈXTIL I D'INDUMENTÀRIA
C. Montcada 12–14
93 310 45 16
www.museutextil.bcn.es
Tues–Sat 10am–6pm;

Sun and hols 10am–3pm
Jaume I
€3.50, free first Sunday
of the month

The city's modern
textile and costume
museum is a sprightly
affair, with a collection
of international fabrics,
embroideries, lace and
tapestries – and an
outrageously camp
display of men's foot-
wear. Also plays up the
impact of Barcelona's
textile industry on the
world catwalk.

PARC DE LA CIUTADELLA
See p.17.

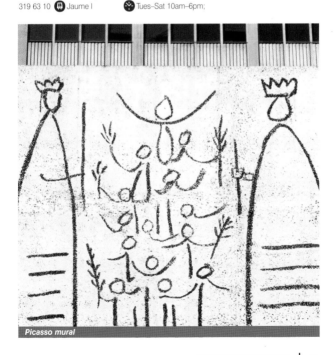

Picasso mural

Terrific Torre (de Telefònica)

Montjuïc

Montjuïc, the monolithic rock that sprawls to the south of the city, is where Barcelona comes to stretch its legs. An oasis of lush parklands with unbeatable panoramas, it is a perfect place for a stroll or a lazy siesta – there's even a network of open-air escalators to help you up and down its steeper flanks.

Rising up from the Mediterranean and unfeasibly close to the city centre, it was here that much of the 1992 Olympic Games were played out.

Montjuïc holds a strong gay fascination – composer Benjamin Britten wrote a dance suite dedicated to it – thanks mostly to its reputation as the city's busiest cruising ground. Not for nothing do the people of Barcelona refer to it as 'Pink Mountain' – its bushes are alive at all times of the day, and the police don't seem to mind.

A DAY OUT

Let's make this easy by starting at the top and working down. But how do you get to the top of Montjuïc? One of the easiest and quaintest ways is the funicular from Paral.lel metro station to A. Miramar, the main road which snakes around the mountain. (*See p.51.*) If you think the views across the city from outside Parc de Montjuïc station are awesome, wait until you pick up the nearby cable car that swings passengers up a stage higher, to the Castell de Montjuïc at the very summit.

The first optional stop-off comes at the Fundació Joan Miró, an impressive white cliff-edge gallery on A. Miramar built to honour the great Catalan symbolist's reputation, with the express intention of housing a large permanent collection of his most important works. It's a must for Miró fans – but there's also a fantastic roof terrace littered with colourful sculptures that are more fun than chin-strokingly 'deep'.

Further along is the Anella Olímpic, the string of sporting complexes renovated for use during the 1992 Olympic Games: namely the Estadi Olímpic, now the home ground of Barcelona's second soccer team, Espanya, and Piscines Bernat Picornell, the awesome laned indoor and outdoor pools that open to the public for lane swimming (don't forget to pack your kit!). The Plaça d'Europa is dominated by architect Santiago Calatrava's dove-white Torre de Telefònica, a futuristic looping telecom tower, with a *trencadís* mosaic at its base, in deference to Gaudí.

The nearby Palau Nacional houses the Museu Nacional d'Art de Catalunya and a tour lays out the nation's stylistic progression from

Monjuïc

9th-century murals discovered in local monasteries, through the birth of Catalan Gothic as an architectural style, and beyond.

Leave the museum and head left, following the signs for the Poble Espanyol, a 1929 educational theme park showcasing each region of Spain with an artisanal 'village' designed in typical local style; it's quite the tourist trap. Alternatively, to the right is the city's busiest cruising area. In the bushes around the Miró-esque glass sculpture, called Arc de Triomf, is where gay men come to lose their invisible dogs in the undergrowth.

Once you've toured either or both fun parks, double back to the front of the Palau Nacional, take a flight of steps down, and you're at the Font Màgica, a monument to kitsch that hosts a popular son-et-lumière show.

Before we reach the bottom, there's more art to be had, not least in the boxy shape of the Pavelló Barcelona, German architect Ludwig Mies van der Rohe's landmark summer pavilion on A. Marqués de Comillas. Over the road, there's the CaixaForum, a newcomer to the Barcelona art scene, hosting important contemporary exhibitions housed in a crenellated Modernista brick building.

Now we're at the foot of Montjuïc. Walk along the gated boulevard A. Reina Maria Cristina, Plaça d'Espanya. The enormous bullring that dominates the far-right exit of the busy roundabout is currently being transformed into a futuristic leisure centre by British architect Richard Rogers. Tournaments are currently held here only occasionally – bullfighting is seen here as a Spanish rather than a Catalan thing – but there's a small museum for those interested in the history of the 'sport'.

☕ Out to Lunch

MNAC restaurant receives unusually good reviews for its relaxed lunch service in a stylish, contemporary restaurant.

Work up an appetite for **L'Albí**, which is inside the Poble Espanyol and does a great €12 *menù del dia* of Med fare, or a series of taster plates (*tastet de la casa*) for €15 to introduce you to the Catalan kitchen: *pa amb tomàquet* (oil-drizzled crusty bread rubbed with tomato, a very typical starter), sausage with beans, vermicelli with shellfish, and so on.

For eats on the hop, try **Bar las Cascadas**, a retro *cafeteria* hut near the Font Màgica that has a limited selection of *bocadillos* but great coffee served by the gruff owner.

CAFÉ FUNDACIÓ JOAN MIRÓ
ⓘ Espanya 📞 93 329 07 68 ⏰ Tues–Sat 10am–6.30pm, Sun 10am–2pm
🚇 Espanya

MNAC
(See p.49.)

L'ALBÍ
ⓘ Inside Poble Espanyol
📞 93 508 63 00
🚇 Espanya

BAR LAS CASCADAS
ⓘ Behind Font Magica
📞 No phone
🚇 Espanya

OUTLINES

MUSEU MILITAR

🛈 Castell de Montjuïc

📞 93 329 86 13

🕐 July–Sept Tues–Sun 9.30am–8pm; Oct–June Tues–Fri 9.30am–7pm, Sat–Sun 9.30am–8pm

Ⓜ Paral.lel, then funicular and teleferic

🎟 €2.40

Perched at the very top of Montjuïc, the former fortress was used as a detention and torture centre for dissenters in the 18th century after the fall of Barcelona. It now houses the last statue of Franco in the city (kept out of spitting distance from have-a-go members of the public). If cabinets of handguns and rifles aren't your thing, check out the peerless city views – and enjoy the precarious cable car ride up here. (*See p.51.*)

FUNDACIÓ JOAN MIRÓ

See p.16.

ESTADI OLÍMPIC

🛈 A de l'Estadi

🌐 www.fundaciobarcelona olimpica.es Ⓜ Espanya, then escalators 🎟 €2.40. Call ServiCaixa for match tickets. (*See p.91.*)

The Olympic stadium is now home of Espanya football club, whose home matches are far easier to get tickets for than the city's favourite, FC Barça. Includes a gallery of Olympic Games–related memorabilia.

PISCINES BERNAT PICORNELL

See p.97.

MUSEU NACIONAL D'ART DE CATALUNYA (MNAC)

🛈 Palau Nacional

📞 93 622 03 60

🌐 www.mnac.es

🕐 Tues–Sat 10am–7pm, Sun 10am–2.30pm

Ⓜ Espanya, then escalators 🎟 €5.50

A brief history of Catalan art, architecture and liturgical artefacts, presented in rough chronological order across 21 galleries in a magnificent mock-Baroque palace. Highlights include the Romanesque murals rescued from Pyrenean churches, and a Gothic collection of religious works commissioned at the height of Catalonia's medieval glory.

POBLE ESPANYOL

🛈 A. Marqués de Comillas 📞 93 325 78 66 www.poble-espanyol.com

🕐 Mon 9am–8pm, Tues–Thur 9am–2am, Fri–Sat 9am–4am, Sun 9am– midnight

Ⓜ Espanya 🎟 €7

Curious that you don't have to leave Barcelona – which hates being called Spanish – for a whistlestop tour of Spain. This theme park

Olympic Stadium

rejoices in Spanish ways of life, with each area represented by a 'miniature village'. There's a bell tower from Zaragoza, a traditional house from Aragon, and so on. Plazas are peppered with lime trees, the smell of garlic wafts out from the rustic restaurants, and feral cats roam about to add Spanishness. As a

MIRÓ'S BLACK MARK

When you're fathoming a colourful canvas by Joan Miró in his Fundació on Montjuïc, think on this: what's behind the meaning of the black asterisk that's a motif in practically every painting he ever did? Nationalists say it's a patriotic stamp representing his allegiance to the 'star of Catalonia'. Nice try – the Catalan star is red. In fact, it's a cheeky signature representing the anus. As a breed, Catalans admit to a slight anal fixation (*see p.35*), and, for Miró, it just shows that even a serious symbolist likes to have his fun…

concept, it's done with a certain élan that should appeal beyond the usual heritage set. But there is a nagging sense that you're paying to walk around a marketplace. Each village has a visitors' workshop selling local handicrafts, such as printed textiles, hand-blown glass or woven baskets. There are smart restaurants, various good-quality terrace cafés, a juice bar and popcorn stands for snacking. And in the summer, the Poble Espanyol stays open late for drinks and, disconcertingly, holds a legendary gay club night on its main terrace. (*See p.88*.)

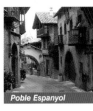
Poble Espanyol

FONT MÁGICA

ⓘ Plaça d'Espanya
✆ 93 291 40 42
www.bcn.es/fonts
✹ Shows every 30 minutes: May–Sept Thur–Sun 9.30pm–midnight; Mar, April, Oct–early Jan Fri–Sat 7pm–9pm
Ⓜ Espanya Ⓥ Free

A mere fountain (albeit a slightly

grandiose example) during the week; on weekend evenings (Thur–Sun in summer) it is spectacularly lit up as the Font's water jets are made to dance and spray to the strains of cheesy pop tracks and classical overtures. Come early to elbow your way to the best vantage point, and prepare to coo and cuddle up to a loved one.

PAVELLÓ BARCELONA

See p.18.

CAIXAFORUM

ⓘ A. Marqués de Comillas 6–8
✆ 93 476 86 00
www.fundacio.lacaixa.es
✹ Tues–Sun 10am–8pm
Ⓜ Espanya
Ⓥ Free

A new gallery inside a renovated Modernista textile mill that houses a collection of European contemporary art, including an installation by Joseph Beuys. Blockbuster retrospectives of internationally renowned artists are also planned, after its opening show of Lucian Freud's was a popular and critical winner.

Joyriding

Part of the fun of Montjuïc is getting there. The number 50 bus is a popular choice – a little too popular in summer, as it's often full by the time it picks up at Plaça d'Espanya. The Bus Turístic and the Tren Montjuïc – not a train but a truck-drawn trolley bus – also wend the same route along the A

Trip to the top

Marqués de Comillas. Both beat flagging cabs at the busy Espanya roundabout. Or you could always walk, leaving the outdoor escalators to take the strain.

More fun is the Funicular de Montjuïc, which leaves from Paral.lel metro, travelling up its own near-vertical tunnel to its own station on A. Miramar. You won't get great views from your seat, but it grinds up the hill in no time. Thrillseekers should then try the teleferic up to the hilltop castle.

And then there's the antique cable car. The Transbordador Aeri whisks tourists, sardine-like in its creaky carriages, from stations in Barceloneta and Port Vell, to the cliff edge near Plaça l'Armada. It's so old – and nail-biting – that it is shut down with the first gust of wind.

TREN MONTJUÏC

ℹ From Plaça d'Espanya to Miramar

📞 93 415 60 20

🗓 Mid April–mid Sept 11am–10pm daily. Every 30 mins

🎟 €1.80 single

FUNICULAR DE MONTJUÏC

ℹ From Paral.lel metro to A. Miramar

📞 93 443 08 59
www.tmd.net

🗓 June–Oct daily 11am–10pm; Nov–April Sat–Sun 10.45am–8pm;

May daily 10.45am–8pm

🎟 €1.70 single, €2.50 return

TELEFÈRIC DE MONTJUÏC

🚠 From Estació Funicular on Av. Miramar to Castell

📞 93 443 08 59
www.tmd.net

🗓 June–mid Sept daily 11.15am–9pm; Mid Sept–Oct, April, May daily 11am–7.15pm; Nov–Mar Sat–Sun 11am–7.15pm

🎟 €3.20 single, €4.50 return

TRANSBORDADOR AERI

🚡 From Torre de Jaume I (Port Vell) and Torre Sant Sebastià (Barceloneta) to Miramar (and vice versa)

📞 93 441 48 20

🗓 Mid June–Mid Sept daily 11am–8pm; Mid Sept–Mid Oct, Mar–mid June daily 10.45am–7pm; Mid Oct–Feb daily 10.30am–5.30pm. Every 15 mins

🎟 €7.20 single, €8.40 return

Surfer sets out

The Seaside

Barcelona's long strip of Mediterranean seaside takes in four neighbourhoods. Port Vell, or Old Port, was once a grim cargo dockland before it was demolished for the Olympic Games and replaced by graceful boulevards lined with restaurants and street sculptures. Barceloneta is the triangular neighbourhood traditionally home to fishermen, before the yuppies started muscling in; there's a swish marina, but cut through the tight-gridded streets to hit the beach and there's a residual working-class flavour. The Vila Olímpica, seafront home to the athletes at the 1992 Games, is now populated by the city's strolling classes, who come for the wide seafront walkways, as well as the shops, restaurants, bars and clubs around the Port Olímpic (there are more nightspots here than in any other part of the city, albeit fairly colour-by-numbers affairs).

The fourth neighbourhood, furthest from the city centre, is Poble Nou (or New Village), a working-class district that is seeking gentrification with the arrival of the 'peace and sustainability expo' Universal Forum of Cultures in 2004 (see www.barcelona2004.org for more details). For now, its greatest asset is its seafront, with beaches seething with sun-seekers in summer, including a nudist section colonised mostly by gays, Platja de Mar Bella, tucked behind the Base Náutica.

As the seafront stretches for four kilometres, consider hopping on a bus. The 41 from Plaça Catalunya will take you to Mar Bella and beyond, while the 36 from the Mirador de Colón gives a comprehensive street-level tour of Port Vell.

A DAY OUT

First things first: make sure you've packed a beach towel and are wearing comfy sandals and plenty of sunscreen. This walk is 10 kilometres as a round trip – so you're guaranteed to catch the sun. Start at the foot of the Ramblas (nearest metro station is Drassanes). Before you hit the beach, it's worth getting your bearings with a trip up the Mirador de Colón, the monument marking the spot where Columbus is said to have landed in 1492 on his return from America – though he's pointing the wrong way (see p.35). If you're lucky, you'll be able to pinpoint a free stretch of beach…

Then you've got a choice. You could walk towards *Cap de Barcelona* (*Barcelona Head*), the landmark Pop Art sculpture by Roy Lichtenstein, along Moll de la Fusta, the palm-fronded waterfront that roars with traffic. Far nicer is to stroll out onto the Rambla del Mar, an 'extension' of the Rambla proper made of wooden drawbridges which swing around to let ships into Port Vell. On a sunny day the wavy walkways – very moderno – buzz with

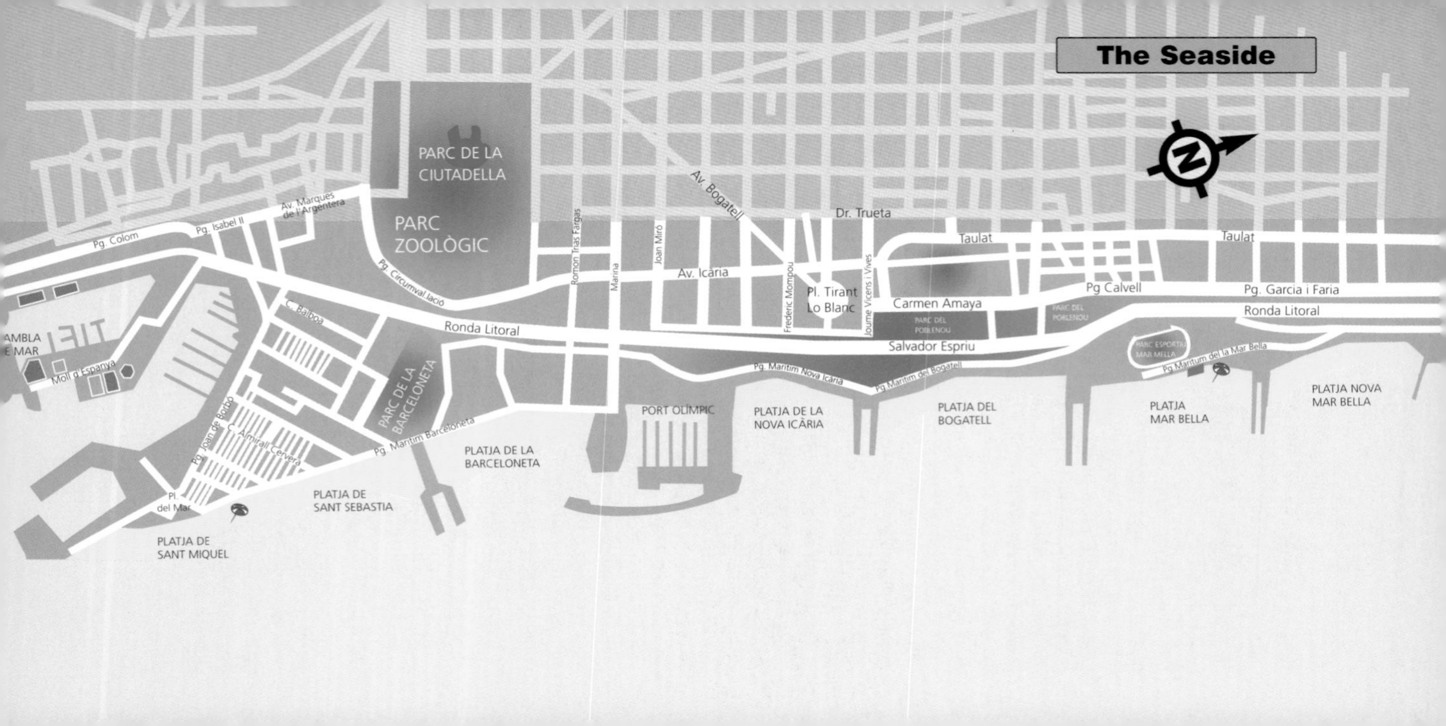

The Seaside

N

PARC DE LA CIUTADELLA

PARC ZOOLÒGIC

PARC DE LA BARCELONETA

Ronda Litoral

Av. Marquès de l'Argentera

Pg. Isabel II

Pg. Colom

RAMBLA DE MAR

Moll de la Fusta

Pl. del Mar

PLATJA DE SANT MIQUEL

PLATJA DE SANT SEBASTIA

PLATJA DE LA BARCELONETA

Joan Miró

Marina

Ramon Trias Fargas

Av. Icària

Av. Bogatell

PORT OLÍMPIC

PLATJA DE LA NOVA ICARIA

Frederic Mompou

Pl. Tirant Lo Blanc

Dr. Trueta

Jaume Vicens i Vives

Salvador Espriu

Carmen Amaya

Taulat

PLATJA DEL BOGATELL

Pg. Calvell

PLATJA MAR BELLA

PLATJA MAR BELLA

Taulat

Pg. Garcia i Faria

Ronda Litoral

PLATJA NOVA MAR BELLA

pedestrians heading for the Moll d'Espanya wharf. This complex showcases attractions like the Maremàgnum shopping centre, an Imax cinema, and Europe's largest aquarium. It is also a popular night-time hangout for clubbers who flock here to its myriad bars and discos.

Once you've been wowed by Moll d'Espanya's shininess and spanking newness, it's time for a gear change. Follow the Moll Dispòsit, past the Palau del Mar which houses the Museu d'Història de Catalunya, around to Barceloneta. The fishing neighbourhood of 'Little Barcelona' is so called because it was created from land reclaimed from the sea in the 18th century. Today, it also houses the pretty Port Vell Marina, whose mooring bays are lined with super-expensive yachts and whose main drag, Passeig Joan de Borbó, is a good place to catch some rays while eating the freshest fish dishes in town (albeit expensively).

At the far tip of Passeig Joan de Borbó, the beaches begin. The Torre de Sant Sebastià on Platja Sant Sebastià is where you can catch the Trasbordador Aeri cable car up to (or down from) Montjuïc. The viewing platform at the top of the station offers great views along the shoreline. At some indiscernible point, Platja Sant Sebastià becomes Platja Barceloneta, which attracts a disproportionate number of same-sex couples amid a sea of oiled-up bodies. The serious posing goes on along the strip near Plaça del Mar.

If you're on a go-slow when walking the length of Platja Barceloneta, admiring the sun-splashed physiques as well as eye-catching beach sculptures as you go, it'll be a good 25 minutes before you reach the Port Olímpic. Alternatively, you can do it double-quick on rollerblades (to hire, visit Al Punt de Trobada in Poble Nou). Aside from the azure-blue sea, sights worth drinking in include Hotel Arts, Spain's tallest building, and its neighbouring 'twin' towerblock; Frank Gehry's fish monument; the street markets, selling cheap ties, knock-off CDs and surprisingly good Louis Vuitton rip-offs; and the shops in the Marina Village stocking essential beach gear. El Centre de la Vila Port Olímpic also has one of the best cinemas for English-language blockbusters, the Yelmo Cineplex – which makes it worth coming back for an evening out. (*See p.92.*)

Once past the port, there's a clear run of well-kept beaches, tree-lined walkways and intermittent bars and restaurants for a couple of kilometres. The beaches are all blue-flag approved for cleanliness, and very well-appointed with showers, deckchairs, beach volleyball courts, lifeguards (in season), and good disabled access. The crowds thin out the further you venture past Platja Nova Icària and Platja del Bogatell. You'll know you're near the gay nudist beach, Platja Mar Bella, when you hit Base Náutica Mar Bella,

Frank's fish

Barcelona's centre for water sports. Head past the groups doing up wetsuits and around the shady hillock that provides some privacy for the only spot in town where you can sunbathe nude.

Out to Lunch

Mango munchies

MANGO
- Platja Nova Icària
- 93 221 35 58
- Ciutadella-Vila Olímpica. Bus 36, 41

XIRINGUITÓ ESCRIBÀ
- Litoral Mar, 42 (Platja Bogatell) 93 221 07 29 . Bus 36 Tues–Thur 11am– 5pm; Fri–Sun 11am–11pm Ciutadella-VilaOlímpica

AGUA
- Passeig Marítim de la Barceloneta 30 93 225 12 72 Mon– Thur 1.30pm– 4pm, 8.30pm– midnight; Fri 1.30pm–4pm, 8.30pm–1am; Sat 1.30pm– 4pm, 8.30pm– 1am; Sun 1.30pm–4pm, 8.30pm– midnight Metro Barceloneta. Bus 45, 57, 59, 157

Barceloneta is famed for its fish restaurants, especially those facing the marina along Passeig Joan de Borbó, a blissful sun-kissed drag that's perfect for a mid-afternoon stroll to peruse the menus. If you're just after drink and snacks (which means sandwiches, cakes and *cortados*) and can't afford to lose that prime spot on the sand, there are three modern beach bars pitched strategically every few hundred metres along Platja Nova Icària, as well as a couple of popular restaurants set back on the promenade. For *fideuà* (Catalan paella), try **Mango**, a popular (if a little soulless) hang-out with hassled staff and outside seating that's manna to bothersome street performers. Near Platja Bogatell is **Xiringuitó Escribà**, a spin-off seafood restaurant from the city's famed Escribà patisserie dynasty. (*See p.61.*) There's a lunchtime tapas menu, and round-the-clock divine desserts, as you'd expect. For fine but informal Catalan dining, ring ahead for a table at Barceloneta's trendiest spot, **Agua**. It has a reasonably priced and popular lunch menu – try the *arròs salvatge amb verdures i gingebre* (wild rice with greens and ginger) – but the deal-clincher is its cool setting right on the beach.

OUTLINES

L'AQUÀRIUM

ℹ️ Moll d'Espanya
📞 93 221 74 74
www.aquariumbcn.com/ing/
index.htm 🕐 Mon–Fri
9.30am–9pm, Sat–Sun (and
holidays) 9.30am–9.30pm
(June, Sept), 9.30am–11pm
July–August 🚇 Drassanes,
Barceloneta 💶 €11.50

The largest aquarium
in Europe where
visitors journey to
the bottom of the
Mediterranean via
a series of glass
walk-ways. Sharks
sporadically flash
their jaws at
excitable visitors.

MUSEU D'HISTÒRIA DE CATALUNYA

ℹ️ Palau del Mar, Plaça
Pau Vila 3 📞 93 225 47 00
cultura.gencat.es/museus/
mhc 🕐 Tues–Thur 10am–
7pm, Fri–Sat 10am–8pm,
Sun 10am–2.30pm
🚇 Barceloneta 💶 €3.01

The marina-edged
attraction rolls out a
visitor-friendly, brief
history of Catalonia in
a series of engaging
and often witty, un-
gallery-like rooms: the
birth and evolution of
the Catalan nation
and people from their
Roman roots to post–
Franco renaissance is
explained in highly
visual terms.

BASE NÁUTICA DE MAR BELLA

ℹ️ A. Litoral (on Platje Mar
Bella) 📞 93 221 04 32
www.basenautica.net,
info@basenautica.net
🕐 Daily May–Sept,
10am–8pm; Oct–April
10am–4.30pm
🚇 Poblenou 🎟️ Individual
prices per activity

Windsurfing, kayaking,
snorkelling, diving,
catamaran sailing…
Barcelona's got it all –
and the Base Náutica
is the one-stop shop
for active waterbabies.
A 20 minute-walk
from the old port,
where Platja Bogatell
meets Platja Mar Bella
(look out for the
rugged types in
wetsuits), come here to
rent canoes, surf boards
and sail boats by the
hour, or for a week's
worth of tuition to
brush up on your
favourite watersport.

LAS GOLONDRINAS

ℹ️ Portal de la Pau
📞 93 442 31 06
www.lasgolondrinas.com
🚇 Drassanes
🎟️ Tours from €3.50 per
person

Tour operator offering
boat trips around the
port and along the
coast. Departures are
every 30 minutes
throughout the day,
from 11.30am to
6.30pm. Booking is

essential. Boats are also
available for hire.

THE ORSOM CATAMARAN

📞 93 225 82 60
www.barcelona-orsom.com,
orsom@barcelona-
orsom.com 🚇 Drassanes
🎟️ Prices on request

Large 90-person
catamaran – the largest
in Barcelona – offering
daily 90-minute
luxury tours of the
port and coastline and
Sunday-night jazz and
banquet cruises.

TRASBORDADOR AERI CABLE CAR

from Torre de Sant Sebastià
See p.51.

HOTEL ARTS

for Frank Gehry's Peix (Fish)
monument
See p.55.

MIRADOR DE COLÓN

See p.55.

IMAX CINEMA

See p.92.

YELMO CINEMA

See p.92.

The Aquarium

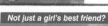

Not just a girl's best friend?

All Shopped Out

Once it was Paris, then New York, and more recently London. Now it seems Barcelona is where Europe comes to shop for the latest fashions. According to reports, 43 per cent of visitors' holiday money is spent in the shops – and there are plenty of places to spend.

From the largest department stores and international fashion brand flagships to the smallest independents dotted along Passeig del Born and Plaça Vila de Madrid, shopping is in Barcelona's blood. Stretch your credit limit further by timing your trip to coincide with the sales (*rebaixes*), which generally run from the second week in January to the end of February, and throughout July and August, when prices are slashed by 50 per cent. In Barcelona, most shops (except department and convenience stores) tend to open Monday to Saturday, from 10am to 2pm, and – following a languid lunch – start reopening around 4.30pm until 8pm. (*See p.144.*)

Top of the Shops

El Corte Inglés

Plaça de Catalunya 14–16 93 306 3800 www.elcorteingles.es Catalunya

Spain's favourite and only true department store, offering everything from gas cookers to groceries under one roof. Though it's a fair way from a thrilling shopping experience, a leisurely stroll around a few of the nine floors will give something of an insight into local life. Like department stores everywhere, the fashion sections will leave most readers of this guide cold, pitched at cardigan-wearers rather than trendsetters. The souvenir shop is best approached with irony.

However, it is particularly strong on sportswear, there's a superb electronics floor where you can fiddle with the latest MP3 players, and the men's underwear section is a revelation. If you can't find Calvins in your size or

The English corner

colour, there are racks of natty Spanish designs like Punto Blanco to tempt you instead. Similarly, the ground-floor perfumery is well stocked with unfamiliar local scents to intrigue a jaded nostril.

El Corte Ingléses are two-a-cent in Barcelona – there's another a minute's walk along Porta de l'Àngel – but this one is a landmark. Eating up a whole block of Plaça de Catalunya, it sits like a majestic white ocean liner in an Art Deco poster (though the façade was actually remodelled in 1994). Even if you're not buying, the views from the 9th-floor Rotonda restaurant across the city are hard to beat – and a great place to down a coffee and re-charge.

Zara

ⓘ A. Pelai 58 **☎** 93 301 0978
Ⓜ Catalunya

The ubiquitous, world-dominating Spanish chain that knocks out catwalk 'fakes' for the masses in record time – from drawing board to shop floor in a matter of weeks – needs no introduction. And especially not in this city, where it's seemingly not against the law – unwritten gay fashion law, that is –

to venture out in public dressed from head to toe in Zara.

The styles, cuts and quality of the clothes are the same as back home – so it's still three washes and you're out – but with up to 30 per cent off UK prices, who's complaining? It does, however, pay to be careful where you buy. The busy flagship on Passeig de Gràcia (No. 245) can be a no-go area at times, so this light, airy, well-stocked store, is a comparative sanctuary.

El Triangle

ⓘ A. Pelai 39　📞 93 318 0108
www.triangle.es　Ⓜ Catalunya

The hulking, visually non-descript mall opposite the El Corte Inglés on Plaça de Catalunya is relatively shy about its merits. Though bland and air-conditioned to the point of sterility, there's something commendably un-high street about its selection of middlebrow shops.

Start at the bottom in Sephora, the largest perfumery in the world. Entry is along a red sloped and mirrored runway that's part catwalk, part gauntlet – either way, a trial of nerves. Once in, it's always teeming with shoppers spritzing themselves with the testers; the written profiles describing the notes in each fragrance are a hoot. Engage one of the shop assistants in conversation and you could walk out with armfuls of free samples.

Come up to ground level for air. Here there are inoffensive mainstream fashions from the likes of Agatha, Dockers, Camper (walls of the quintessential Catalan deck shoe and variations on that theme), Massimo Dutti (for contemporary and fitted men's workwear), and Desigual, a unisex fashion outlet with borderline-outrageous printed gear. Also noteworthy is the FNAC, whose strongest suits are its CD, book and magazine departments, complete with the latest English-language publications.

El Triangle

Escribà Confiteria i Fleca

ⓘ La Rambla 83
📞 93 301 6027
Ⓜ Liceu

It's the remarkable blue Modernista mosaic covering the shop front that first attracts the eye – the windows of this dazzling corner bakery are filled with sweet delights – but it's the trays of glistening chocolates and cakes that drags you over the threshold. The Escribà Confiteria i Fleca is a one-stop choc stop-off for those on their way to pastry heaven, and the famous resident patissier, Antoni Escribà, could build a stairway to it out of meringue or chou, so heady are his towering confections shaped like world landmarks. As you're filling a box with goodies to take back to the hotel or scoff on a bench on the Rambla, ask to see the latest masterpiece he's working on out back.

For an even better reason to stop by and blow the diet, there's a café at the rear. And if the waistline says you should stay away, beware: the team also run Xiringuitó Escribà, a remarkable seafront restaurant near the gay beach. (*See p.56.*)

ALL SHOPPED OUT

Vinçon

🛈 Passeig de Gràcia 98   📞 93 215 6050   www.vincon.com   Ⓜ Diagonal

OK, so you might not be in Barcelona to buy a new dining suite or a dinky bookcase for the spare room, but sometimes you've got to go beyond Elle Décor to piece together a new look. And no place does inspiring Catalan interiors quite as well as Vinçon, the city's most stylish home outfitters.

Naturally enough, it's full of well-heeled gay couples ignoring the designer brats springing on the mattresses in the bedding section. Done up like a moody black-walled art gallery, presumably to justify the top-rung prices as much as to give you an idea of how icons of 20th-century design might look once you get the flatpack home, this showroom of style is a one-off. Still, you could always take back a desirable picture frame, a set of nibble bowls or an interesting corkscrew (made in Denmark, probably) as a memento of your trip to the design city.

Ovlas

🛈 Via Laietana 33   📞 93 268 7691   Ⓜ Jaume I

Just round the corner from the Cathedral La Seu is – holy of holies – an emporium dedicated to in-your-face gaywear. The gear here is own-label, complete with rainbow-tag branding, and much of it carries a distinct whiff of SM. This is where the gay underground look goes overground. There's loads of black leather and PVC, but it's worth stocking up on T-shirts here as they come in every colour, size and fit.

Though the glass-fronted boutique is unapologetically high street, the beary staff plays up the menaces. But that doesn't deter nervous heterosexual couples popping in to look for a kinkier than usual piece to wear to the club or in the bedroom. It's full of gear for special occasions rather than wardrobe staples, and its designs are playful and just about wearable – like the jeans with tracksuit edging. Once you've seen the size of the bill you've just run up, you'll need a stiff drink at the on-site café-bar.

Ovlas

Shop Around

FASHIONWEAR

ANTONI MIRÓ
🛈 A. Consell de Cent 349
📞 93 487 0670
www.antoniomiro.es
Ⓜ Passeig de Gràcia

Toni Miró is to Catalans what Jean-Paul Gaultier is to the French – their local designer-done-so-good that every gay Barcelonan wants him in their wardrobe. He's your scissorsmith if high-quality, off-the-peg contemporary menswear in that muted Mediterranean palette – black, beige and cream – is your look.

AWC ALTERNATIVE CLUB WEAR 2
🛈 Galería Citadines, A. Plaça Vila de Madrid
📞 93 317 7413
Ⓜ Liceu

Smaller boutique to its big brother on A. Riera Baixa, stocked with a hand-picked selection of gorgeous goodies from the wearable mens - and womenswear collections (Seal Kay seems to be a favourite). Rifle through rails of funky trews, dyed leather jackets, great knits and one-off tees. Great cases of chunky bracelets and retro watches, too.

BAD HABITS
🛈 A. de Valencia 261
📞 93 487 2259
Ⓜ Passeig de Gràcia

Still doing the gypsy look? There's plenty of loose-legged, high-volume and nicely embroidered pieces on the racks at this favourite of ethereal, Mother Earth lesbians. Mind your head as you go down the steps on your way in.

COOL HUNTER
🛈 Passatge del Duc de la Victoria 5 📞 93 302 3778
Ⓜ Liceu

A small and oh-so stylish, in-the-know emporium sparsely stocked with pieces from the more exclusive, edgier Eurochic designers: DSquared, Vivienne Westwood and Dries Van Noten.

CELESTINA MUÑOZ
🛈 Gran Via de les Corts Catalanes 538
📞 93 453 9817
Ⓜ Universitat

Looking for something special for a night out? Be sure to make a detour to this quiet, middle-of-nowhere boys' boutique, which does a neat line in unusual trainers, sophisticated shirts and unrestrained printed tops.

ALL SHOPPED OUT

CUSTO BARCELONA

🛈 Plaça de les Olles 7
☎ 93 268 7893
Ⓜ Jaume I

The high-fashion label that's a favourite with the stylists at *Shangay* magazine, judging from its appearance in almost every fashion story. Designer Custodio Dalmau's exclusive boutique in the Born district has the craziest patterned tops, psychedelic long-sleeved tops and body-hugging sweaters. For show-offs who like to make an entrance.

DIESEL

🛈 Corner of Passeig de Gràcia and A Diputació
☎ 93 317 0535
Ⓜ Passeig de Gràcia

It's a staple in every gay and lesbian wardrobe, and all your favourite lines are here (although no cheaper than at home). But should you fancy your nth piece of Diesel denim, you'll be glad you popped by.

KWATRA

🛈 A. Antic de Sant Joan 1
☎ 93 268 0804
www.kwatra.com Ⓜ Jaume I

The first unibrand store in Spain – in the cutting-edge Born district, naturally enough – selling the coolest Nikes, with carefully selected tops and bottoms from of-the-moment names that mix and match to compliment the footwear.

LACOSTE

🛈 Rambla Catalunya 72
☎ 93 487 0739
Ⓜ Catalunya

A belatedly gay label from France – something to do with that 2002 poster campaign with a naked male model – the store in Barcelona stocks

Diesel time

designs exclusive to
Catalonia. Drop by to
pick up a special Polo
shirt for dad.

SO_DA

A. de Avinyó 24
93 412 2776 Liceu

Antonius . . .

One of the trendiest
streets in the Barri
Gòtic, limited editions
rule. The only place in
Barcelona to find the
diaphanous designs of,
say, Stella McCartney
and Yohji Yamamoto's
Adidas strap-up fashion
boot. At night, the
collections are locked
away and the doors
flung open for fashion
happenings, with DJ
sets and cocktails.

SPIKE ACTION

Plaça Vila de Madrid 5
93 412 2759 Liceu

Great range of disco
tees (Levi, Replay), gay-
boy vests in all sizes,
Diesel swimwear,
jackets and jumpers. In
short, a one-stop kit
shop for clubbers who
can't be seen out in the
same thing twice.

SECOND-HAND GEAR

RECICLA RECICLA

A. Riera Baixa 13
93 443 1815
Sant Antoni

Where dedicated

followers of flea-market
fashion rummage
alongside fans of Sergio
Tacchini originals.

MIES I FELJ

A. Riera Baixa 5
93 442 0755 Liceu

Large and well-ordered
selection of second-
hand denim, with Levi's
a speciality.

MUSIC AND BOOKS

ANTONIUS

A. Josep Anselm
Clavé 6 93 301 9070
www.antinouslibros.com
Drassanes

A thoughtful, contemp-
orary lesbian and gay
bookshop in Barri
Gòtic, which doubles as
an information centre.
Run by a quietly
dedicated staff (who'll
give you the lowdown

on gay Barcelona), it's a
great place to browse –
there's a small selection
of English-language
books – and occasional
events in the café. But
the biggest thumbs-up
is for the stock of gay
magazines and listings
guides.

DISCOS BALADA

A. Pelai 24
Universitat,
Catalunya

This bargain-basement
CD store can be a hit-
and-miss affair, but it
often throws up the
occasional gem. It pays
to dig: as well as the
latest chart releases,
there are always
absurdly low offers
on back catalogue
CDs – anyone for a
long-forgotten Prince
3-CD set for €5? –
plus great box sets
and an interesting
classical selection.

Heavenly nightspot

FNAC

See El Triangle (p.61).

EL CORTE INGLÉS

ⓘ Portal de l'Àngel 19
☎ 93 306 3800
Ⓜ Catalunya

Comprehensive ground-floor CD and DVD department at the satellite of the nearby flagship branch in Plaça Catalunya (*See pp.59–60*.)

HOME INTERIORS

DOM

ⓘ A. Avinyó 7
☎ 93 487 1181
www.id-dom.com
Ⓜ Liceu

Barcelona is full of middlebrow interior shops selling superior home décor (and a fair share of pointless space-fillers). At least the buyer at this one has the well-to-do homo-at-home in mind. It's also presided over by pretty-boy assistants who seem to enjoy giving gay customers a knowing look. If you don't want to walk out with a fun plastic shower curtain, wire magazine rack or a nest of moulded perspex tables, there's also a selection of rare imported chillout CDs which you can sample before you buy.

MARKETS

ELS ENCANTS

See p.27.

SWEET THINGS

M BOMBÓN

ⓘ Comte d'Urgell 61
☎ 93 454 9244 Ⓜ Urgell

Great place for inventive chocolate gifts and modern boxed goodies. There's the usual selection of street tiles (complete with nutty underlay) inspired by Gaudí designs, or wackier gifts like the planets of the solar system recreated in swirly marbled chocolate. Also a good place to stop for a hot chocolate or *refresco*. Popular with well-to-do ladies who shop, while Macy Gray CDs provide the chilled soundtrack. Friendly mumsy staff.

GAY SHOPS

BLACK

ⓘ A. Consell de Cent 235
Ⓜ Universitat

Possibly the world's trendiest gay sex store – more like a contemporary art gallery than a shop selling the usual vids, mags and paraphernalia.

SESTIENDA

ⓘ A. Rauric 11 ☎ 93 318 8676 www.sestienda.com
Ⓜ Urgell

One of Barcelona's first sex shops, still giving good, discreet service. There are plenty of booths for you to fast-forward through your selection of vids before deciding.

ZEUS

ⓘ A. Riera Alta 20
☎ 93 442 9795
Ⓜ Sant Antoni

Slightly awkwardly located sex shop stuck in a busy immigrant area of the Raval. Still, a great place to pop in for a browse or to pick up the *Shanguide* gay listings mag.

SHOPPING MALLS

MAREMÀGNUM

ⓘ Moll d'Espanya, Port Vell
☎ 93 225 8100
www.maremagnum.es
Ⓜ Barceloneta

The smoked and mirrored glass exterior of this monolithic mall complex on the port edge shrouds little mystery inside. It's the predictable run of uninspiring low-rent clothing stores, family or theme restaurants and tourist tat shops.

Time for tapas

Eating Out

Barcelona eats late. Unless you enjoy being first into restaurants or dining alone, synchronise your stomach rumbles with the Catalan clock. Lunch is an unhurried affair, soaking up the hours between 2 and 4pm (and then it's siesta, so plenty of time for another coffee…), while dinner is served no earlier than 9pm (and often at midnight). Around 6pm, the city decamps to a *granja* for a pastry pick-me-up and milky hot drink, or to a tapas bar for something quick on a stick over a beer.

Visitors are pleasantly surprised by how easy it is to eat well and cheaply in Barcelona. Lunch is better value still if you ask for the *menú del día* (menu of the day) rather than ordering à la carte. For a choice of several starters, entrées, a dessert, bread and a drink, expect to get change from €10. Barcelona's foodie scene is as internationalist as the city itself.

Cream of the Cuisine

Castro

ⓘ C. Casanova 85
☎ 93 323 67 84
🕒 Mon–Fri 1pm–4pm, 9pm–midnight; Sat 9pm–midnight Ⓜ Urgell 🖂 🈁

Gay restaurants come no more elegant than this – though there's not a frilly tablecloth in sight, and the only jacket required is a leather one. The décor is industrial chic, the walls are charcoal and gun-grey, with concrete columns wrapped with

The following price guides have been used for eating out and indicate the price for a main course:

🈁 = cheap = under €7

🈁 = moderate = €7–€17

🈁 = expensive = over €17

chains – imagine dining in a softly-lit sex dungeon – and the sense of theatre palpable: once coats are taken, they are handcuffed to the stand. The serious, black T-shirted staff, with their regimented authority and inside-out knowledge of the menu, add to the sub-dom atmosphere.

But this is no S&M theme restaurant – it's one of the best places to eat in town. Accordingly, there's a mix of dining gourmets (though most are moustachioed), and all are smart but not stuffily dressed for the occasion; put on your best leather trews for a night here. In spite of the upmarket sleaze feel, it's not so much a gay restaurant as a restaurant that's gay. The ingenious menu sparkles. Warm rolls and *fuet* (spicy Catalan

sausage) come as cover, and there's an impressive prix fixe with four choices for each course. For starters, the *sopa fría* (chilled soup) is like frothy milk laced with melon chunks; the carpaccio is well paired with pear and nuts.

The playful Catalan spirit is much in evidence in the main course selection; the grilled veg platter comes with courgette, carrot, pineapple and kiwi in the skins and rind – an excellent surprise (though rather dented by the undersized portion). Carnivores might like the pork with goat's cheese.

The service is defiantly not flappy, but competent and helpful. Ask for assistance with the wine list, a toss-up between the local reds from Penedès.

Cuisine at Castro

Jaume de Provença

ℹ C. Provença 88 **☎** 93 430 00 29 **❤** Tues–Sat 1pm–4pm, 9pm–11.30pm, Sun 1pm–4pm **Ⓜ** Entença **Ⓥ** **Ⓦ**

With the décor time-locked in the 1970s – and not in a knowing, tongue-in-cheek retro way – fads in Catalan cuisine have washed over this Gràcia bolt-hole (est. 1942), which teeters on the edge of fashionability by being resolutely impervious to its swings and roundabouts. In keeping with the height of the prawn-cocktail-years ambience, the menu champions 'market cooking' and is typified by good old steak and mushrooms (albeit wild ceps). It's a good place to splash out for a mini-celebration with friends – the *menu degustation* for €52 per person kicks off with a cleansing avocado cappuccino, and includes house specialities like pork trotters, lobster and rosemary roasted lamb. There's also a cheaper menu of supposed seasonal Catalan goodies that proves the local kitchen's magpie tendencies, as it includes *bacalão con all-i-oli de mangos* (strips of cod done Basque country style, served with mango mayo) and *mousaka de conejo confitado* (rabbit moussaka). A la carte mains start at €12 and promptly rocket – as do prices on the decent wine list.

Botafumeiro

ℹ Gran de Gràcia 81 **☎** 93 218 42 30 **❤** Daily 1pm–1am **Ⓜ** Fontana **Ⓥ** **Ⓦ**

Seafood fans take note: this is widely considered the best restaurant for fish in town – as the waiting list attests. If it swims, you're pretty much guaranteed to be able to eat it here, served up in typical Galician (rather than Catalan) style. With a restaurant of this size – some 300 covers set out impeccably in a Baroque banqueting hall – and an international reputation to live up to, the waiters in gold-trim white uniforms are drilled for their part in what amounts to a nightly military manoeuvre; service can border on the brisk and intrusive. But come here for the menu, not the table-side manner. Specialities include oysters, lobster and langoustines – which you can earmark from a tank of dozens – as well as fish and meat stews. The enormous list of Galician white wines begs to be sampled.

if you prefer, the takeaways are substantial

Seltz

ℹ️ C. Rosselló 154 📞 93 453 38 42
⏰ Wed–Sat 9pm–3am
Ⓜ️ Hospital Clinic 🌐 🏳️‍🌈

This vermouth bar is at the vanguard of a club-cum-restaurant trend that has swept Barcelona: think of it as a dancerie-eaterie. Have an aperitif at the counter, then as the DJ warms up, try some trendy tapas from the select menu of *platitos*, small side dishes of the chef's own invention. And when the tables are cleared away, dance it all off to hard house. Definitely a concept not to be missed – and the illuminated frosted flooring decorated with Campari labels is very Saturday Night Fever.

La Flauta Magica

ℹ️ C. de Banys Vells 18 📞 93 268 46 94
⏰ Mon–Thur, Sun 8.30pm–11.30pm, Fri–Sat 8.30pm–12am Ⓜ️ Jaume I 🌐 🏳️‍🌈

A loudly decorated boho hangout in Born, popular with a hardcore trustafarian element who read out scenes from their latest screenplays at the recital nights every Thursday. While not strictly meat-free (its cuts are organic), it has some of the choicest veggie platters, which draw inspiration from the world over. The mushroom crêpe is a winner, and the sushi on the picture menu (served at weekends only) looks inviting. Will you be joining the in-crowd for Sri Lankan curried rice or corn fritters from Venezuela?

Jupiter

ℹ️ C. Jupi 4 📞 93 268 36 50 ⏰ Tues–Thur, Sun 7pm–1am; Fri–Sat 7pm–2am Ⓜ️ Jaume I
🌐 🏳️‍🌈

This place is a nightmare to find, hidden in a seedy backstreet off Via Laietana at the back of the main post office, but, wow, what a find! A gay-run left-field lounge restaurant popular with manga-comic reading grungers, the décor gives a good indication of the playfully inventive menu that awaits. There are bamboo decorations on the walls, a chill-out bit with reconditioned settees and 70s coffee tables – and a main eating area. *Bocadillos* and salads provide the main ballast to the nibble-friendly menu, and no dish is more than €8. The portions are small and satisfying, which makes it easy to try as many dishes as you can from the extensive list.

The shaded terrace of Tèxtil Cafe

Café Miranda

ⓘ C. Casanova 30
📞 93 453 52 49
🕙 Daily 9pm–1am
Ⓜ Universitat 🏳️‍🌈 ♿

Barcelona's first drag restaurant, this sister to the flagship (dragship?) in Madrid has been packing them in ever since it opened its velvet drape-covered doors. The professional cabaret performers (drag queens, dancers, acrobats and even trapeze artists) do their best to detain you from your meal with their high-octane, highly polished routines. There's such a buzz about the place, and it's a fixture both in the gay listings mags and the reviews pages of local papers, so straight diners also flock here for a kitsch night out. Secure a table well in advance, especially at weekends when last-minute bookings will have the accommodating front desk pulling their (own) hair out.

Tèxtil Cafe

ⓘ C. Montcada 12 🕙 Tues–Sat 10am–8pm, Sun 10am–3pm Ⓜ Jaume I 🏳️‍🌈 ♿

Madrid-Barcelona

Madrid-Barcelona

ⓘ C. d'Aragó 282 🕙 Mon–Sat 1pm–3.30pm, 8.30pm–11.30pm
📞 93 215 7027 Ⓜ Passeig de Gràcia
🏳️‍🌈 ♿

Most nights of the week, especially weekends, and even during lunch, there are patient queues outside this 1920s marisco bar located on the old Madrid to Barcelona railway line (it was part of the former station). Appropriately, the menu is a fusion of Spanish and Catalan favourites, though the *pa amb tomàquet* (bread rubbed with tomato, a Catalan speciality) served with steamed mussels and chunky fish soup gets the juices flowing fastest.

This smart courtyard café at the Museu Tèxtil i d'Indumentària has plenty to recommend it. The cool, shaded terrace is dressed with conservatory furniture, offers great veggie options – there's a whole page in the menu devoted to meat-free mains, and plenty of starters to weigh up, too – but here's the deal-clincher: expect to pay €20 per head for three courses, coffee and a brandy or two.

Shamelessly geared towards tourists, it falls shy of pulling in coach-loads of the baseball-capped masses, but it's something of a highlight in one of the Barri Gòtic's most popular attractions. Try a comforting 'taste of home' plate containing typical Spanish, Italian, Lebanese, Japanese (and so on) fare, or sandwiches named after the cities associated with the fillings, like a pastrami and rye (New York) and London's BLT (or bacon, lettuce and tomato). In fact, its only major downside is that it's not open late enough for dinner – unless your stomach has yet to acclimatise to continental meal times.

Best of the Rest

Bracafé

BRACAFÉ

ⓘ C. de Casp 2

📞 93 302 30 82

🕙 Open 7am–10.30pm daily ⓜ Catalunya

💳 🍽 Cash only

An always-crammed Brazilian coffee bar with amazing Art Deco fittings and possibly the strongest brews in town. Choke down your *cortado* with second-hand smoke inside – or grab a table in the street, just off Passeig de Gràcia. Mind those shopping bags, though…

CASA CALVET

ⓘ C. de Casp 48

📞 93 412 4012

🕙 Mon–Sat 1pm–4pm, 9pm–11pm ⓜ Urquinaona

💳 🍽

Set in the gorgeous interiors of Antonio Gaudí's first commissioned apartment building in Barcelona, this ought to be a tourist trap; it's the only place in town where you can eat inside a Modernista landmark. But its enduring reputation for fine Catalan/ Mediterranean with a twist has been secured by the elegant setting and local inventive favourites such as oyster ravioli dressed with foamy Cava-laced sauce.

CAL PEP

ⓘ C. de les Olles 8

📞 93 310 79 61

🕙 Mon 8pm–12am, Tues–Sat 1.15pm–4.15pm, 8pm–12am

ⓜ Barceloneta 💳 🍽

Antiquated fish joint that's lorded over by a convivial owner. Popular with hardy Barceloneta locals, who sup on the best fruits of the sea caught that day.

LA VERÒNICA

ⓘ C. Avinyó 30

📞 93 412 11 22

🕙 Tues 8pm–1.30am, Wed–Sun 12am–1.30am

ⓜ Jaume I 💳 🍽

Radical pizzeria with blonde wood tables and a loud paint job, where lipstick lesbians come to hold court over a wild mushroom salad or two.

ANTIGUA CASA SOLÉ

ⓘ C. Sant Carles 4

📞 93 221 50 12

🕙 Closed Sunday nights and Mondays

ⓜ Barceloneta 💳 🍽

For seafood that cries out to be photographed as well as a treat to eat. Book yourself in for a languid Sunday afternoon lunch of *arroç negre amb sepia en su tinta* (literally, 'black rice with squid in its own ink').

GOVINDA

ⓘ Plaça de la Vila de Madrid 4–5

✆ 93 318 77 29

✺ Variable times

Ⓜ Catalunya

Veggie Indian with weekly changing menu of *paneers, dhals, koftas* and *Bengali sabji* – with occasional screwball options like enchiladas to remind you that you're in Spain. There's also a well-replenished salad bar. Worth calling before turning up as it tends to keep raggedy hours.

COMME BIO

ⓘ Gran Via de les Corts Catalanes 603

✆ 93 301 03 76

✺ Daily from 2pm

Ⓜ Passeig de Gràcia

A vegeterian botega with an inspiring way with textured proteins like tofu. Great salad starters, and the killer main is the risotto marina made with tofu, seaweed and smoky ceps. It's pricy, the décor's not up to much, and waiters are unrushable and on the dopey side. A minor find for grateful health foodists.

TENORIO

ⓘ Passeig de Gràcia 37

✆ 93 27 20 592/94

✺ Daily 7am–1am

Ⓜ Passeig de Gràcia

Swish and stylish are the passwords at this international brasserie for the designer shopping fraternity. This place is power-dressed straight out of the 80s (that's Catalan irony for you). There's purple dark wood and chrome everywhere, lit large by enormous arc lights. If that's too much theatre, snag a table on the terrace, where prim portions are served on frosted glass plate-bowls.

TRAGALUZ

ⓘ Passatge de la Concepció 5

✆ 93 487 06 21

✺ Mon–Wed, Sun 1.30pm–4pm, 8.30pm–12am; Thur–Sat 1.30pm–4pm, 8.30pm–1am

Ⓜ Diagonal

Tucked in an Eixample side street, this colourful resto-bar with a planet-arium-like glass roof is great for fine, informal dining – and stargazing. The *menu degustation* comes in at €49.60, or for simple finger food choose between club sandwiches, hamburgers and fajitas. There's a good veggie selection, too. All the fittings here are designed by Javier

International cuisine

Mariscal, creator of 1992 Olympic mascot, Cobi.

LA DIVA RESTAURANT

ℹ️ C. Diputació 172

📞 93 454 63 98

🌙 Mon–Sun 9pm–12am; show at 11pm (Thur–Sun)

Ⓜ️ Universitat

Another drag restaurant – Barcelona foodies love their 'amuse girls' – the pretender to Café Miranda's throne. Come for the show, rather than the food.

LA SINGULAR

ℹ️ C. Francisco Giner, 🌙 From 8pm (closed Sundays)

Ⓜ️ Fontana

Where the girls are. Swinging lesbian-run and owned restaurant in Gràcia, which packs them in. Good international food, great, warm ambience.

TOMATE

ℹ️ C. dels Sombreres 17

🌙 Mon–Thur 12pm–11pm; Fri–Sun 12pm–12am

📞 93 315 1048

Ⓜ️ Jaume I

A neat cucina vegetariana in the Barri Gòtic where you eat surrounded by lotus lampshades and pictures of Vishnu. The unbeatable lunchtime buffet and salad bar is €7.

GRANJA M VIADER

ℹ️ C. Xuclà 4–6

📞 93 318 34 86

🌙 Daily 9am–1:45pm; 5pm–8:45pm

Ⓜ️ Catalunya

Well-to-do *granja* bar packed with Catalan ladies with good hairdos and their pipe-smoking partners. Part of Barcelona's fabric, the original owners' medals are proudly displayed around the walls, alongside reviews from newspapers through the ages.

CAFÉ TORINO

ℹ️ Passeig de Gràcia 59

📞 93 487 75 71

🌙 Mon–Thur, Sun 8am–11pm; Fri, Sat 9am–1.30am

Ⓜ️ Passeig de Gràcia

Cash only

Popular corner café bar in the Eixample, with a striking curved-beamed entrance. A handy stop-off when doing the Modernista sights on Passeig de Gràcia.

Popular corner café bar

AMALTEA

ℹ️ C. Diputació 164

📞 93 454 86 13

🌙 Daily 9am–10pm

Ⓜ️ Urgell

Cash only

Deli-front café in the Gaixample with a great veggie *menú del día* for €8.

BAR FORTUNY

ℹ️ C. Pintor Fortuny 31

📞 93 317 98 92

🌙 Tues–Sun 10am–midnight

Ⓜ️ Catalunya

Cash only

Perfect for a quiet sit and smoke as you wait for your unfussy home-cooked meal to arrive. A popular lesbian bodega, stacked with old barrels and funkily decorated with toy robots, though you still get the odd elderly gent walking in for the dinner, too.

RESTAURANT FINDER

Local drink, Cava

As you eat your way through mountains of fresh fruits of the sea and other delights from the Barcelona kitchen, think: what to wash it down with? The answer is cava, the Catalans' response to champagne. This sparkling white wine is aged in underground cellars (*cava* means cellar in Catalan), and is drunk by the glass to celebrate no occasion whatsoever; treat yourself to a glass first in the early evening. Sipping a chilled flute is as common here as

Cava – celebrate life

pint – downing is in London – and it's a good look for gay bars. Look out for Freixenet and its long-time rival Codorniu – or head for a pre-clubbing tipple with the trendies at El Xampanyet, a buzzing Cava palace.

EL XAMPANYET
🛈 C. Montcada 22
📞 93 319 70 03 ☀️ Daily
6.30pm–11.30pm Ⓜ Jaume I

SALVATION
GAY DISCO

xxixx
do gay

music bar
EFLEJOS

ra. 19   Sitges

LE MALE A BAR

CENTRO
COMERCIAL
OASIS
LOCAL

Out on the Town

So Barcelona hasn't got the biggest scene in the world, or even in Spain – that's one distinction that goes to Madrid and its village, the Chueca. And variety isn't the spice of gay life here, either. The upmarket style bars in the Left Eixample, or Gaixample, are often high-concept variations on a well-shaken cocktail: a young, trendy crowd, designer décor, and €5 plus for a spirit and a bottle of mixer.

But the city has plenty for gay partygoers to write home about, not least its attitude – or rather the lack of it. Less up itself than London and New York, the vibe is fashion-conscious but come-as-you-are, to the extent that gays and lesbians happily welcome each other into their bars (the boys are mostly in Gaixample; the girls congregate in Gràcia). Some of the gayest hangouts – like the after-hours clubs (after 6am) – aren't officially gay, but you wouldn't know from all that hugging…

My Top Clubs

Metro

🛈 C. Sepúlveda 185 📞 93 323 52 27 www.metrodiscobcn.com
🕖 Daily midnight–6am Ⓜ Universitat 💲 €10 (plus free drink). Free passes handed out at Café Dietrich

In a town where what's hot changes with every issue of *Nois* magazine, Metro is a rare institution, impervious to the whims of fashion and packing them in with its formula of unpretentious pop you can bop to. Whether they like to admit it or not, it's every boy's favourite club. The main dance floor is a hands–aloft mix of current hits from the European and American charts, while the second delves into the disco archives – but not too far back; Las Ketchup's *Asereje* is guaranteed to be played nightly. Ricochet between the two floors as soon as you can – once the place picks up at 3am, it'll be so busy you won't want to move around. Clubbing doesn't come any sweatier than this.

Need a rest? There's chilling out to be had around the pool table, and there's always plenty of queues to join. Those for the gents' toilets are legendary: perhaps it's something to do with the monitors above the urinals that play porn on a loop… Midweek drag shows pull in a boisterous mixed crowd, and look out for the occasional foam parties, which are also legendary. Thanks to an unimaginably confusing layout, many a lost clubber has also been known to stumble upon the spacious darkroom and porn chamber. Whatever you're into, Metro is a must for the sheer fun factor alone. Don't leave town without trying it.

Café Dietrich

🛈 C. Consell de Cent 255
☎ 93 451 77 070
🕙 Daily 6pm–2.30am (Sat 3am)
Ⓜ Universitat

As the name suggests, the city's most famous gay bar has a slight German accent. The first thing you'll notice, waltzing past the bouncers and through dramatic thick red drapes, is the enormous cartoon portrait of Marlene, striking her classic pose, but haggard to the point of grotesqueness, her pendulous, age-withered carriage grazing her knees. *Wilkommen*, as they say, to Barcelona's tongue-in-cheek taste of Berlin.

Style is the name of the game here, a mix of contemporary beige and Art Deco fittings strewn with giant plants. There's a narrow slipway lined with mirrors and stools – perfect for hanging with a drink while pretending not to be taking a good look at new arrivals. The long, L-shaped bar, which is watched over by an attractive T-shirted crew who have among their ranks some of the most attentive servers in town, leads to a raised dance floor at the back. Dietrich is all about getting in the mood to move on elsewhere, so there's a rosta of DJs on deck duty, getting the party started. But that's only the half of it.

This being Barcelona, the dance area is intermittently cleared for drag performers to mouth their way through mini routines. And this being Dietrich, the entertainment goes that little bit further than the local norm. Throughout the night, go-go boys dance on whatever podiums they can make available, while the occasional fire-breathing circus act wows the crowds in the ornamental garden.

You don't go out in Barcelona without stopping by Dietrich first. And it's worth popping in for the free passes to Metro. On Friday nights it's full of new faces, lads (and the occasional lass) from all over the continent, straight off the plane, getting busy chatting each other up in Spanish, French, Dutch, or whatever. Now that's the kind of European union Marlene would approve of.

The famous Café Dietrich

Punto BCN

C. Muntaner 63

93 453 61 23

Daily 6pm–2.30am

Universitat

Like La Rambla, during a trip to
Barcelona you will end up in
Punto at some point – usually
sooner rather than later. For this is
the early bird's bar of choice.

Anyone who's out for the night
rocks up here for their first drink
of the evening – which is
everyone from the slew of tight
T-shirted disco bunnies who
stream in constantly, to the older,
pipe-smoking men in cardigans
with dogs on leads who never
seem to arrive or leave. All types
in between are invited, too – and
happily that also includes women.

Though it's a boys' bar, there's
always a healthy flow of lesbians,
as well as a few straight girls in
tow (wherever those disco bunnies
go…).

One of the first heavy-hitting
bars on the block to open, it's
cavernous, airy, and with air-con
so strong it could snuff a match –
so at least you won't step outside
reeking of smoke. The look is
unthreateningly anodyne –
Americana meets Eurostyle –
with a long bar decorated with
Budweiser ads, Coke ads and
Molson neons. Though there's
enough floor space for an army of
friends, it fills quickly, making it
an easy spot for strangers looking
to look inconspicuous. If you are
on your own, hang back by the
mini art gallery, and before long
you'll be engaged in conversation.

Alternatively, hang round the pool table upstairs.

As Punto is run by the same group as the Arena clubs (which are predominantly heterosexual nowadays), with every drink you'll be handed discount flyers. A better bet, free passes to Salvation disco are handed out at about 1.30am on Fridays and Saturdays.

Bright decor at Átame bar. (See p.86)

Salvation

ⓘ Ronda Sant Pere, 19–21
🌐 www.matineegroup.com
🕑 Fri–Sat and festival days
midnight–5am 🚇 Urquinaona
🎟 €10

The gay disco that all Barcelona wishes it could gatecrash. But despite being bang in the non-gay heart of the city, it's almost strictly men only. Only a handful of hand-picked female plus-ones are plucked from the long queues outside every night.

So what's the fuss about? First, there's an on-the-money aficionado's room for guest DJs playing quality dance, which is packed all night with gyrating bodies. And for those with less upscale musical tastes, there's an equally busy modern trash and retro floor with a fun line in

Europop. On Friday nights there are live spectaculars, but there's no getting away from the fact this is, basically, a slightly harder-core version of Metro. The magic's working, though – bouncers have been turning away straights since it first opened in 1999. It's worth hunting down the flyers which offer free entrance on Fridays, and reduced door damage on Saturdays and holidays.

Martins

ⓘ Passeig de Gràcia, 130
📞 93 218 71 67 www.discomartins.com
🕑 Daily midnight–5am
🚇 Diagonal
🎟 €8

This fabulous dinosaur is so old, the Gaixample didn't exist when it first opened at the 'wrong' end of Passeig de Gràcia some 20 years ago. (Back then, the Sagrada Família, a few blocks away, would have looked very different.) But it's easy to see why this cruisy ultra-late venue has not only survived, but thrived.

Impervious to the fickle finger of fashion, Martins is where men come to play, especially when nearby bars like the Eagle and New Chaps have chucked out for the night. The vibe is suitably heavy, reflected in the industrial, warehousey look. There's little by way of relief from the black painted walls, unless you count the one-way mirror in the gents' toilets which allows you to watch newcomers arrive as you stand at the urinal.

A late-night pick-up joint, there are dark areas and a loft playing porn on a big screen. Oh, there's also a dance floor for those who want it. On an off night, when it's not busy, it's easy to rattle around Martins, cavernous as it is. But hold out for the delegation of pneumatic transsexuals that inevitably, and inexplicably, arrive for a dance with the jackboot and leather fraternity. At Martins, everyone's welcome, tourists especially. Look out for flyers, which offer free entry until 4.30am.

G Café

🛈 C. Muntaner 22
🕿 No phone
🕑 Mon–Fri 4pm–2.30am, Fri–Sat 6pm–3am
Ⓜ Universitat

The 'G' in the name is for 'gay', and also for 'Gaudí'. Stands to reason, as God's architect has inspired the look and the vibe at this small but unique bar. Like its namesake, who was passionate in his attention to detail, the décor borders on the devotional. The bar itself looks like a Gaudí offcut, its coloured animal mosaics undulating like the benches in Park Güell. In contrast, the walls are stark white and hung with crucifixes, with church candles leaking wax over every table top. With the solemnity tempered by touches of Catholic kitsch, this place feels

like a temple. This is the height of the alternative gay scene in Barcelona, and seems all the more outré for its flouting of the city's modern bar design conventions. Here, all the furniture is perversely odd, a hotchpotch of random dining chairs, chaise longues and armchairs in need of re-upholstering. Behind the bar, there's a small selection of drinks; the best spirits and the owner's favourite beer – which means it feels like you've been invited to a salon.

Open for civilised chilling during the afternoon siesta, when there's an easy soundtrack of well-chosen lounge compilations, at night it becomes a dance bar presided over by a low-key ambient DJ. Tables are simply pushed aside to make way. But whether you hit the floor or prefer to curl your feet up to relax, it's so informal, it's your prerogative. Out of the way on the outer limits of the Gaixample – but it's worth getting out the map to find.

Bright lights along the beachfront

Caligula

ℹ️ C. Consell de Cent 257 📞 93 451 48 92 Ⓜ️ Universitat 🕐 Daily 10pm–3am

Small, intimate and done up like a gladiator's rest, this heady and exotic bar could well be the perfect place for getting quietly sloshed with friends. The décor is your first talking point, a low-lit Roman orgy of velvet drapes, scattered petals and flickering candlelight. Pity the poor slave who has to light all the tea lights dotted around the room.

Order a bottle of rioja from your waiter (handsome in their regulation black Tees rather than togas), and enjoy the gentle classical or chillout soundtrack. Then, just as you're nearing the last drop, the lights go down and it's cabaret time. From behind a curtain, out slinks an is-she-isn't-she trannie who mimes her heart out to a Celine Dion track while the bar boys studiously work spotlights, dry ice and a wind machine. It's quite a performance, up close and very personal. Have a few more bottles and they'll also be punctuated with intermittent performances.

There's something divinely decadent about Caligula, which attracts an easy-come mix of guys and girls. It's attitude-free, great for unwinding with mates or a lover, and the attention to detail is superb. They've not forgotten the bathrooms either, where there's smashing black hand soap resting on banana leaves. All that's missing is the orgy!

Clubbing scene

Z:eltas

ℹ️ C. Casanova 75
📞 93 454 19 02 www.zeltas.net
🕐 Daily 10.30pm–3am Ⓜ️ Urgell

The vibeyest, most fashion-conscious meeting point pulls in a dressy crowd of all ages and persuasions. The long, narrow bar – a riot of exposed brickwork, painted murals and plasma screens playing pop videos – is perfect for posing. Further along, it opens out into a dance area, which gets busy after 1am. If you're staying a while, it's worth checking your coat in at the back while there's still space.

Best described as a place for friends rather than friendly. The clientele can be on the cliquey side, although the smiley bar staff do their best to keep everyone happy. If you're waiting on your own, there are plenty of gay magazines to graze. Pull up a stool and nurse an enormous house measure, or slouch out on the cream sofas.

The bar feel gives way later to a clubbier vibe. Before you head off to Metro or Salvation, remember to take the flyers being handed out at the door, offering free passes to after-hours clubs. In Barcelona, you never know where a night will lead…

Ironic Café

ℹ️ C. Consell de Cent 245

📞 627 92 98 53

🕐 Tues–Sun 7pm–2.30am

Ⓜ️ Urgell, Universitat

Quiet until well after midnight, this is one of the less crazed bars on the gay beat. Trendy but without the fashion police, it's a convivial place to carry on a post-restaurant conversation with friends – there's a video wall but you can still hear yourself speak. Sample the great liqueur selection or take your time with one last coffee; their *cortados* (espresso with a shot of hot milk) come with a little pastry. For those heading for bed, there's the widest selection of *infusiones* (herbal teas) you'll find anywhere (the *manzana y canela* is highly recommended), while those looking for a pick-me-up will find a long list of sexy cocktails to get them in the mood. Take your pick from Libidinous Asia, Red Wet Lips, and Green Shower.

Aire Sala Diana

ℹ️ C. València 236 (between C. Balmes and C. Enriq Granados)

📞 93 451 84 62

www.arenadisco.com

🕐 Thur–Sat 11pm–3am; Sun (women only) 6pm–10pm

Ⓜ️ Passeig de Gràcia

🎟️ €3 (Sat €6, includes one drink)

the parties here swing with sounds of the past, but there's enough contemporary pop and house thrown in to keep the more fashion-minded dyke happy. It's strictly women only on Sundays (there's even an early-evening strip show on the first Sunday of the month), though throughout the rest of the week men are welcome as guests.

Barcelona's biggest and busiest lesbian venue pulls in more than 300 women most nights. Part of the Arena group (who also run Punto BCN (*see pp. 81–82*), this is a suitably stylish and unpretentious girl dance bar. As the Saturday Night Fever coloured dance floor suggests,

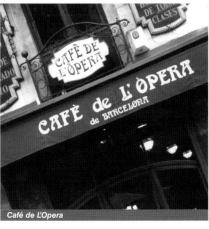
Café de L'Opera

All Clubbed Out

AMBAR

ℹ️ C. Casanova 71
📞 93 451 59 94
🕐 Daily 6pm–3am
Ⓜ️ Universitat

All-day lounge bar, in the heart of the Gaixample, with chillout sounds until 11pm, then harder house until closing.

ARENA CLASSIC

ℹ️ C. Diputació 233
📞 93 487 83 42
www.arenadisco.web
🕐 Fri and Sat only 12.30pm–5am
Ⓜ️ Universitat
💳 €5 Fri, €9 Sat

The best of the Arena group disco attracts a fun-loving crowd lapping up anthems from the 70s, 80s, 90s and right now, and gets cheesier as the night goes on. A refreshingly unpretentious mix of lesbians, gay men and mates makes this the ideal big Saturday night out for groups.

ÁTAME

ℹ️ C. Consell de Cent 257
📞 93 454 92 73
🕐 6pm–2.30am, Fri–Sat 3am
Ⓜ️ Universitat

A one-drink-then-move-on kind of place, with an odd mix of hustlers and couples engaged in intimate conversations.

BACKSY CAFÉ

ℹ️ C. Diputació 161
📞 93 451 52 58
🕐 Daily 10am–2.30am
Ⓜ️ Urgell

Straight-acting multi-screened video bar, with gorgeous barmen and screens everywhere playing a mix of terrestrial TV, football matches and gay porn. Magazine racks are stuffed with *Men's Health, Zeus* and the weekend supplements. Thursday happy hour 9–11pm, with two for one drinks. Breakfast and lunch also offered.

COCK RING FORMERLY CAFÉ DE LA CALLE

ℹ️ C Viç 11
📞 93 218 38 63 🕐 Daily 6pm–3am Ⓜ️ Fontana

Renamed, and no longer a light and airy lesbian bar, Cock Ring now caters to a heavier male crowd. Not for a girls' night out – even though it's in the dykey Gràcia district.

CAFÉ DE L'OPERA

ℹ️ La Rambla 79
📞 93 317 75 85 🕐 Mon–Thur, Sun 8am– 2.15am; Fri–Sat 8am–3am
Ⓜ️ Liceu

A mixed straight/gay (in that order) coffee shop with a long history as a hangout for post-performance opera queens. By day, it does great tapas, though it's best to skip the seats on the street and the upstairs overspill, and claim a doorway table instead (great for people-watching on the Rambla).

DANZATORIA

🛈 A. Tibidabo

Ⓜ Tibidabo

The latest thing: a dance bar set in the grounds of a mansion house on Tibidabo, with an enormous dance area in the backyard. Mixed straight/gay, unlike its white-trash sister club in Port Olímpic, but very gay at weekends.

DAPHNES

🛈 C. Consell de Cent, 223 📞 93 323 30 82

🕥 Sun–Wed 8am–midnight; Thur–Fri 8am–3am; Sat 5pm–3am

Ⓜ Urgell

A very friendly, tiny café-bar dressed in swathes of purple and animal-print furnishings that's never busy but always open. Great place to eat or drink quietly with friends.

D BLANCO

🛈 C. Villaroel 71

📞 93 451 59 86

Ⓜ Universitat, Urgell

www.d-blanco.com

Style bar – all in white – with good selection of salads and 'dedicated' sandwiches. Never busy, though.

EAGLE

🛈 Passeig de San Joan, 152 📞 93 207 56 58

www.eaglespain.com

🕥 Fri–Sat 10pm–3am; Sun–Thur 10pm–2.30am

Ⓜ Verdaguer

Where Bearsalona comes to play. A dress-code bear pit for guys into jeans, leather, rubber, uniform, and the rougher side of life. There's a busy dark-room, and occasional theme nights, including underwear-only sessions.

FREE WOMEN

🛈 C. Casanova 43

🕾 No phone Ⓜ Urgell

🕥 Sun–Thur 4pm–1am; Fri–Sat 4pm–2am

A cosy lesbian café serving drinks in a laid-back gallery space.

NEW CHAPS

🛈 A. Diagonal, 365

📞 93 215 53 65 🕥 Mon–Thur 9pm–3am; Fri–Sat 9pm– 3.30am; Sun 7pm–3am

A meeting place and playpen for guys into leather and denim. There's a busy labyrinth and dark room. On Sunday afternoon there's also a happy hour, with two for one drinks.

OUI CAFÉ

🛈 C. Consell de Cent 247

📞 93 451 45 70 🕥 Sun–Thur 5pm–2am; Fri–Sat 5pm–3am Ⓜ Universitat

Popular meeting place with lots of cosy

Backsy Café – one of the city's many leather bars

Wilkommen to Café Dietrich

crannies, especially popular with guys who don't look old enough to drink. Serving coffee and cocktails from early evening, with a neat outdoor terrace in summer. The staff could show more interest in customers other than their regulars, though.

LA PEDRERA DE NIT

ℹ C. Provença 261
☏ 93 484 59 95
www.funcaixacat.com
Ⓜ Diagonal 💲 €10

The unparalleled rooftop bar at Gaudí's La Pedrera is a dressy hangout in the summer months. Not gay, but popular with gay locals and tourists alike. Beware the steep entry fee.

LA ROSA

ℹ C. Brusi 39, Plaça Molina ☏ 93 414 61 66

⏱ Thur–Sun 10pm–3am
Ⓜ Fontana

The first ever lesbian bar to open in Barcelona, in the Sant Gervasi district, is now an older women's haunt. It remains a welcoming, neighbourhood bolthole, if a little out of the way, with gentle music and a genteel, discerning clientele. Great for surreptitious hand-holding over a glass of wine.

SCHILLING

ℹ C. Ferran 23
☏ 93 317 67 87
⏱ Mon–Sat 10am–1.30am; Sun noon–2.30am
Ⓜ Liceu

Mock Viennese coffee bar popular during the day with intellectual homos, and with barflies at night. Noisy and smoky.

SOUVENIR

ℹ C. Noi del Sucre 75, Viladecans (outside Barcelona), A-16 motorway (exit 50)
☏ www.matineegroup.com
⏱ Sat, Sun, and before festival days, from 5am
Ⓜ No metro; RENFE train to Viladecans

Barcelona's best after-hours gay club that's not even in Barcelona! A motorway-side warehouse serving up banging house to a wasted crowd.

LA TERRAZA CLUB

ℹ A. Marques de Comillas, Poble Espanyol
☏ 93 423 12 85
www.nightsungroup.com
⏱ Thur–Sun (May–Oct only) midnight–6am
Ⓜ Espanya

As the name suggests, it's a large open-air club on a palm tree-lined terrace in the Poble Espanyol *(see pp. 49–50)* serving up house to a mixed, up for it, posey crowd. Drag shows at weekends, when it's gayest. A real Barcelona experience, and one of the best and biggest clubs in town, so it's worth going once just to say you've been. Summer months only.

Barcelona/Sitges events

Not sure when's the best time to visit Barcelona and Sitges?
The place goes a shade pinker than usual three times a year.
First, during the Sitges Mardi Gras, a traditional and wild street
carnival held in the seaside town every February in which gay
locals play a visible part. Then, if you're lucky and Barcelona's
gay burghers have got their act together, there's a national Pride
event at the end of June (though it supposedly alternates with
Madrid). Check if it's going ahead, and in which city, in the news
section of the www.gay.es website, or in the local gay press.
More dependable is the annual International Lesbian and
Gay Film Festival, an established calendar highlight held in
Barcelona every October/early November. Check
www.festivalbarcelona.com for details. And remember to
book accommodation in advance, as demand is even
higher during such events.

A night out

Cinematic wonder

Playing Around Town

Barcelona's performance art scene is as varied as the stars it has brought to the international stage: from opera legends José (Josep in Catalan) Carreras and Montserrat Caballé, who occasionally perform at the splendidly renovated Liceu theatre, to its sparkiest theatrical troupe, Els Joglars.

When it comes to cinema, Barcelonans are fanatics, and the city has everything from local fleapits to state-of-the-art multiplexes, as well as an IMAX in the port. Wherever you go, tickets generally are cheaper on *el dia del espectador*, usually Mondays and Wednesdays, and often for the first showing of the day.

Tickets for most performance events are available from the ServiCaixa hotline (902 33 22 11). For detailed listings, newsstands sell the weekly *Guía del Ocio*, or check out the comprehensive Exit section of the daily *El Periódico*.

But if it's free street theatre you're after, every Sunday morning outside the La Seu cathedral in the Barri Gòtic, ageing locals put on a display of Catalonia's unintentionally hilarious national dance, the *sardana*.

OUTLINES

GRAN TEATRE DEL LICEU

La Rambla 51–9
902 33 22 11
(ServiCaixa)
www.liceubarcelona.com
Liceu. Bus: 14, 38, 59
Tickets €6.50 to €150

One of the greatest opera houses in Europe and now one of its most technologically advanced, the Liceu has twice been rebuilt after major fires, reopening in 1999 after its most recent misfortune. Tickets for the star-studded performances are hard to come by. But the schedule is dotted with semi-staged performances and recitals of interesting lesser works, often by Catalan composers, which are sometimes easier to attend.

Imax in the port

TEATRE NACIONAL DE CATALUNYA

ℹ️ Plaça de les Arts 13
📞 933 06 57 00
www.teatrelliure.com
🚇 Monumental, Glòries.
Bus: 6, 7, 10, 56, 62
🎟️ Tickets from €12.50
to €19.50

A grand public theatre inaugurated in 1997 to bring a spot of culture to the run-down Glòries area. A glass temple perched on a sweep of steps, it's as impressive outside as in, with two auditoriums in one complex. The programme runs the gamut from Greek tragedies to new Catalan commissions.

YELMO CINEPLEX

ℹ️ C. Salvador Espriu 61, Vila Olímpica 📞 93 221 75 85 www.yelmocineplex.es
🚇 Ciutadella-Vila Olímpica
🎟️ €5.60

This unremarkable shopping mall complex deserves a mention for its late-night showings (*madrugadas*) on Fridays and Saturdays. With 15 films – mostly Hollywood blockbusters with Spanish subtitles – it is a haven for cinema buffs and insomniacs alike, and you can always go out clubbing afterwards or drink in the nearby marina. Be prompt because the screens sell out quickly.

IMAX PORT VELL

ℹ️ Moll d'Espanya
📞 93 225 11 11
🚇 Barceloneta, Drassanes. Bus: 14, 36, 57, 59, 64, 157 🎟️ €7–€10

A mix of Spanish, Catalan and English language giant-screen showings (some in 3D), including a couple of midnight sessions.

PALAU DE LA MÚSICA CATALANA

ℹ️ C. Sant Francesc de Paula 2 📞 93 268 10 00
www.palaumusica.org
🚇 Urquinaona. Bus: 17, 19, 40, 45

A remarkable Modernista building that hosts the most prestigious events in the city's classical music calendar. Highlights include an annual guitar festival, and every 26 December, *Sant Esteve*, a showpiece classical concert that's a sellout and broadcast live on Catalan television. The acoustics are notoriously bad, sacrificed on the altar of Modernista aesthetics. Take in the latter on a pre-concert guided tour.

CINES ARENAS

ℹ️ C. Tarragona 5–7
📞 93 423 11 69
🕐 Daily from 4pm
🚇 Espanya

Tucked behind Hotel Plaza, this low-key cinema plays arty Spanish and Latino movies with a gay flavour – like Ralf Koenig's interpretation of Lisístrata – and occasional racy Super 8 flicks in the main auditorium. If you can't follow the action, there are more hardcore goings on in the porno bar.

MÉLIÈS CINEMES

📍 C. Villaroel 102
📞 93 451 00 51
🕐 Tues–Sun
🚇 Urgell. Bus: 14, 20, 38, 59
🎫 €4.20; Mon €3

Cinephile heaven: a two-screen rep cinema showing *versió original* (original version) films, mostly big-screen classics and arthouse

staples with Catalan or Spanish subtitles. Regular double and triple bills keep the film buffs coming back.

INTERNATIONAL LESBIAN AND GAY FILM FESTIVAL

www.festivalbarcelona.com

The Festival Internacional de Cinema Gai i Lesbic is held in Barcelona every October in venues across the city, screening queer film from around the world. During the 10-day festival, bars and clubs in the

Gaixample throw lively party events.

FONT MÁGICA

See p.50.

PALAU SANT JORDI

📍 A. de l'Estadí
📞 93 481 11 92
🚇 Espanya, then escalators. Bus: 50

If it's live pop music you're after, all the big names like Madonna, Whitney and Pink have played this high-tech sports hall. In 2002 it hosted the MTV Europe Music Awards.

Box office beyond the average

Try pedal power . . .

Working Out

Got calories to burn? It's easy in Barcelona. New York-style gym chains have landed and locals are smitten. Gays and straights alike proudly carry their kit in the nifty string bags from DiR fitness clubs. If treadmills aren't your thing, join the rollerbladers along Platje de la Barceloneta, try your hand (and upper arms) at La Foixarda, an urban climbing wall up on Montjuïc, or go sailing from the Base Nàutica (93 221 04 32, www.basenautica.net) that marks the start of the gay beach, Mar Bella. Alternatively, you can hire a bike (*see p.96*), or take a two-wheeled guided tour of the city. Packages are offered by Mike's Bike Tours (93 301 36 12, www.mikesbiketours.com) and Biketours by Biciclot (93 307 77 475, www.biciclot.net). Runners can happily train along the relatively flat seafront, or, for tougher terrain, on Montjuïc or Collserola, the hill opposite. Both tough inclines are included on the route of the Marathon Catalunya, held in Barcelona every March (www.redestb.es/marathon_cat).

OUTLINES

METATRON

- C. Aribau 131
- 93 419 97 48
- Mon–Fri 7am–11pm, Sat 12pm–3pm, 6pm–9pm, Sun 6pm–9pm
- Hospital Clinic. Bus: 14, 31, 38, 54, 59, 63, 66
- Day membership €10, week €25, month €75

Barcelona's leading gay gym attracts serious body builders, general keep-fitters of all shapes and ages, and professional go-go boys who spend their days pumping and preening to a soundtrack of Kylie remixes and underground house. Here, the equipment is well-worn and the cardiovascular section limited mostly to cycling machines, but the atmosphere is friendly and concentrated. It is busiest after 6pm, when it also gets cruisier. Classes include Body Pump, Tai-Chi, Step and Body Combat. Most staff speak English.

Enter the Metatron

Well-equipped gym

DIR EIXAMPLE

ℹ️ Passatge Domingo 6–8
📞 93 450 48 18. General
DiR info: 901 30 40 30
www.dirfitness.es
🕐 Daily 7am–11pm
Ⓜ️ Passeig de Gràcia.
Bus: 24, 43, 44, 54, 64, 66, 67, 68
💶 From €22.84 to €76.63 a month. Other rates on request

Not gay but a popular Barcelona-wide chain with the set who like to sweat in style. This branch on the edge of the Gaixample has a large work-out room, massage rooms, steam bath and walk-in solariums, plus more than 80 classes from aerobics to cardio kickboxing.

LA FITNESS

ℹ️ Bruc 122
📞 93 208 1444
www.lafitness.co.uk
Ⓜ️ Diagonal, Passeig de Gràcia, Verdaguer. Bus: 6, 15, 20, 33, 34, 43, 44, 45, 47
💶 Day membership €12. Other rates on request

The British chain recently opened in Barcelona, mostly attracting a business crowd. Popular with guests from the nearby Hostal Qué Tal (*see p. 125*).

AL PUNT DE TROBADA

ℹ️ C. Badajoz 24
📞 93 225 05 95
bicipuntrobada@hotmail.com
🕐 April–Sept, daily 9am–3pm, 5pm–9pm; Oct–Mar, Mon–Sat 9am–2pm, 4pm–8pm, Sun 9am–5pm. Ⓜ️ Llacuna. Bus: 32, 92
💳 AmEx, MasterCard, Visa

Bike hire shop with friendly, knowledgeable staff, perfectly placed in the Poble Nou district for a spot of cycling along the seafront. Mountain bikes and

rollerblades from
€3.60/hour,
€10.80/half day,
€16/day.
Tandems also
available.

PISCINES BERNAT PICORNELL

🛈 A. de l'Estadi 30–40, Montjuïc

🌀 93 423 40 41
www.picornell.com

☀ Mon–Fri 7am–midnight, Sat 7am–9pm, Sun 7.30am–8pm (Oct–May, Sun 7.30am–4pm)

🚇 Espanya, then escalators; Paral.lel then funicular. Bus: 50, Bus Turístic

💳 €8 (€4.50 June–Sept). Cash only

Built for the 1970
European swimming
championships and
dolled up for the
Olympics, Montjuïc's
impressive twin pools
(the outdoor pool is
heated in winter) are
easily the best place to
do laps in the city.
Consider the 20-
minute walk up the
hill from Espanya
metro station as your
warm-up. The indoor
pool hosts nude
sessions after hours on
Saturday nights and
Sunday afternoons
(call for more details)
and there's a weights
room attracting a fair
proportion of gay
men and lesbians.
Staff speak little
English but are
friendly.

SAUNA GALILEA

🛈 Calàbria 59

🌀 93 426 79 05

☀ Mon–Thur 12pm–midnight, then 24hrs; Fri 12pm–Sun midnight

🚇 Rocafort, Poble Sec

💳 €11

Not far from the
Gaixample, Galilea
attracts a mix of ages
and sizes with its
clean sauna and steam
rooms split over four
floors. The five-man
Jacuzzi on the top
floor is a popular
secluded spot. The
myriad private cabins
have videos on loop.
Busiest days are cut-
price Tuesdays and
Thursdays, when it's
full of students.
Weekend mornings
6-9am, entry is
reduced and includes
free breakfast.

SAUNA CASANOVA

🛈 C. Casanova 57

🌀 93 323 78 60

☀ Daily 24hrs

🚇 Hospital Clinic, Urgell

💳 €10

Barcelona's busiest
sauna is an acquired
taste. The dirty
perspex water chute
that decorates the
entrance stairwell isn't
the most pleasant
welcome, but once
inside it's a clean
enough place.
Towels and slippers
are included in the
price and the door
staff are friendly
and speak good
English, but the
clientele are
notoriously sniffy.
Busy yourself in the
darkened sauna and
steam rooms, or
watch TV and chat in
the chill-out lounge.

Casanova, cleaner on the inside

Sant Bartomeu i Tecla on the Sitges skyline

Sitges

A guide within a guide

Stepping Out

A 20-minute train ride from Barcelona's Sants station, down the Costa Garraf, is the historic seaside resort of Sitges (pronounced Seet-yes). Its narrow cobbled streets, beautiful buildings, 7 kilometres of wide Mediterranean beaches (17 in total) and shallow shoreline – oh, and same-sex couples from all over the world holding hands without a care – make Sitges a must–do for any visitor to Barcelona.

A popular retreat and party town for avant-garde artists in the late 19th century (Picasso and his set chilled out here), the town retains a cultured sparkle, even though its palette is decidedly rainbow-coloured these days. In summer there's even a special 'pink night-train' that shuttles tired revellers back to Barcelona during the small hours. Ask at the station or tourist information office on C. Sínia Morera (93 894 42 51, www.sitges.org).

My Top Sights

Església de Sant Bartomeu i Tecla

🛈 Plaça de la Església
☀ Open only during Mass: Mon–Fri at 7.30pm, Sat 8pm, Sun 9am–12pm

The most iconic landmark in Sitges, this 17th-century church dominates the skyline, staring out over the Mediterranean from its promontory. The original steps leading up to the church were eroded by the sea, though the church itself remains defiant against the elements. Local legend has it that fishermen's wives used to climb the bell tower to watch out for their returning spouses. Perhaps from here you can pick out yours along the 4 kilometres of beachfront to the east. While its location and views are more arresting than its interior, the impressive Baroque organ has its admirers. The church becomes a focal point during the town's Festa Major celebrations in August, in which locals parade *gegants* (giant puppets) through the streets before a superb firework display.

Street of museums

Museu Maricel

ℹ️ C. Follonar 🌞 Summer: Tues–Sun 10am–2pm, 5pm–9pm. Rest of year: Tues–Fri 10am–1.30pm, 3pm–6.30pm, Sat 10am–7pm, Sun 10am–3pm
💶 €3 (or entry to all three Sitges museums, €5.45). Free first Wed of the month

Just beyond the church, the Palau Maricel was commissioned by an American millionaire and Sitges devotee Charles Deering to house his art collection from medieval times – including Romanesque wall paintings and altarpieces – to Renaissance wood-carvings and 20th-century works. Constructed by Miquel Utrillo, the palace (once a hospital) is ornately tiled and has several magnificent terraces. The mirador, considered by many as the highlight of the museum, offers a breathtaking sea view and explains why the palace is named after sea and sky (*mar i cel*). From June to September, it hosts popular midweek summer night concerts.

A Marques de Montroig

Sitges's gayest drag – which isn't saying much – this café-lined strip leading to the beach becomes a catwalk by day, colonised by gay boys and girls sipping lattes while eyeing up the passing talent through dark glasses. Everyone seems to decamp here for the siesta – great for people-spotting. If this is café central, then C. de 1er de Maig, the street it feeds into across the Plaça de la Industria, is gay clubland. With its banging gay clubs, it is better known locally, albeit ever so respectfully, as Sin Street. To swap admiring glances in the afternoon, pitch up early at the Café de Montroig (*see p. 108*), whose terrace offers the most eye-catching vantage point.

Platja de la Bassa Rodona

Though the entire Sitges beachfront is friendly, tolerant, and mixed, the stretch in front of the Calípolis Hotel is the biggest gay draw; you'll find the highest density of stripped-down gay men and lesbians here during the

Promenade

day. The gazing at toned and tanned bodies is unsubtle, and the atmosphere friendly and social rather than intimidating. A 10-minute stroll along the beach from Sant Bartomeu church, it's where everyone gathers in high season to dissect the adventures of the previous night; if you made an impression on the scene, expect tongues to be wagging as you rub in your sun lotion. There are sun loungers for hire and showers for getting the sand out of those awkward places. Look out for the families of friendly wild cats miaowing around the piers.

Platja del Home Mort

Sitges's delightfully named gay nudist area – Playa del Muerto in Spanish, or Dead Man's Beach – is a hike and a half, pitched some 4 kilometres from the main gay beach, and involves an element of orienteering. Wear sensible shoes and be prepared for an hour's power-walking.

Walk the length of the Passeig Marítim sea front to the Hotel Terramar (or catch the Bus Urbà from the station, which terminates here). Continue along the rocky beach if the tide is out, or follow the road to L'Atlàntida Disco; a cab from the town centre to this, the last reachable point by transport, costs €7. Now climb the hill path and walk along the railway. Stay on the sea side of the railway for the path to the beach, or cross over to the woods to join the other gay men resting in the shade.

The first beach is the mixed nudist beach; keep going for another 10 minutes to Platja del Home Mort which is almost exclusively for gay men. In high season, a shack serves expensive cold drinks and snacks – as this is quite a trek, it's a captive market. The beach is pebbly, so rent a lounger or bring a big towel.

Now, there is an easier way to sunbathe nude in Sitges. There are a couple of designated beaches to the left of Sant Bartomeu church, but naked bodies here tend to attract stares from tourists at the Mirador. Might be worth an hour's walk to Platja del Home Mort, after all…

Beach with a view

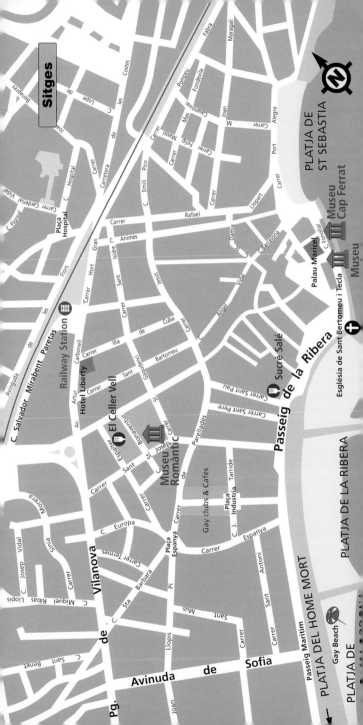

Sitges: Around Town

A DAY OUT

There are few must-sees in Sitges. But thanks to strict planning regulations, the narrow, twisted streets of the Old Town remain timewarped, with rows of whitewashed matchbox-style houses and pretty plaças. Simply walking around is to be immersed in traditional Catalan character.

Those coming to Sitges for the buzz and the beachlife will want to stake their place on the sand as soon as possible. They should follow the crowds streaming off the *rodalies* (local train) from Barcelona – its streets are so tight, and the ride so easy, you'll be glad you left the hire car behind (*see box p.104*) – along all routes downhill to the Passeig Marítim. As you pass, make a mental note of Carrers Espalter, Bonaventura and Bonaire; with their numerous gay clubs and bars, these are the backbone of the gay scene.

Those here for a bit of sightseeing rather than just copious sun should head from the station along C. Artur Carbonell to pick up the local gay listings guides and maps at the Hotel Liberty. (*See p.128*.) Take a left into Sant Francesc, and you'll arrive at Plaça Cap de la Vila, the small main square – so small there's barely room for a Smart car to swing around it.

From here, those interested in the Museu Romàntic – which lays bare the life of a wealthy 19th-century family in Sitges in a series of recreated period rooms – can head up C. Sant Francesc. Otherwise, it's on to C. Major, Sitges's shopping high street with its chic boutiques and not excessively tacky souvenir shops.

This leads us to Plaça del Ajuntament, whose neighbouring alleys house the town's two other collections, the Museu Cap Ferrat and Museu Maricel. But the crowning glory of this neighbourhood – literally – is the towering Església de Sant Bartomeu i Tecla in Plaça de la Església (*see pp.99–100*). Come back to experience Mass – all day Sundays – and get access to the rooftop for fantastic views.

Now it's time to hit the beach. Platja de la Fragata and Platja de la Ribera both have volleyball nets. But for somewhere to catch the sun and be seen rather than exert yourself, walk along the wide seafront, Passeig de la Ribera, to the gay beach, Platja de la Bassa Rodona (*see pp.100–101*). To lose the crowds, head further down the snaking beachfront. There's a gay nudist beach about an hour's trek from here. (*see p.101*).

When you've had your fill of the sun, head up C. 1er de Maig, which is referred to inexplicably as Dos de Maig and feeds into C. Marqués de

Montroig, the drag of gay cafés that's packed with life all summer. Pull up a seat (again, space permitting) or just lean with a bottle of Dos Equis and start posing. Only a matter of hours till the clubs open…

Hit the beaches for a game of Volleyball

GETTING TO AND AROUND SITGES

To get to Sitges, take the **train** from Barcelona-Sants station. A single ticket is €2.10 and trains leave every 20 minutes, usually from platforms 5 and 6 (look for trains to Vilanova). The journey takes between 20 and 30 minutes, depending on stops.

With its narrow streets and tight corners, Sitges is particularly vehicle-unfriendly – here, the pedestrian is king. The C-31 route from Barcelona also tends to be congested (the expensive toll route, C-32, less so). Ever get the impression that the Catalans want you to use public transport?

A good way to do the seafront is on two wheels. **Cycles** are for hire from €9 a day at La Bicicleta (Centre Comercial Oasis, tel 93 894 87 58). The terminally lazy can call a **taxi** in Sitges on 93 894 35 94 or 93 894 13 29.

OUTLINES

MUSEU ROMÀNTIC

ⓘ C. Sant Gaudenci 1 🕿 93 894 29 69
🕐 Mid June–mid Sept, Tues–Sun
10am–9pm. Mid Sept–Mid June Tues–Fri
9.30am–2pm, 4pm–6pm; Sat 9.30am–
2pm, 4pm–8pm; Sun 9.30am–2pm
💲 €3 (or entry to all three Sitges
museums, €5.45)

See how aristocratic Catalans lived
at the end of the 19th century, at
the height of the *Renaixença*
(Renaissance), with a peek inside
this purposefully preserved family
home. Guided tours, offered every
hour, reveal a grand
Mediterranean house that was
built with rich architectural
flourishes – there's an impressive
main stairwell – that's decorated
rather more modestly by its less
extravagant former residents.

MUSEU CAP FERRAT

ⓘ C. Follonar
🕿 93 894 03 64

🕐 Mid June–mid Sept Tues–Sun
10am– 9pm. Mid Sept–Mid June Tues–Fri
9.30am– 2pm, 4pm–6pm; Sat 9.30am–
2pm, 4pm–8pm; Sun 9.30am–2pm
💲 €3 (or entry to all three Sitges
museums, €5.45)

Art buffs can shade from the sun
in this former home and art
studio of Santiago Rusiñol, a
leading light of Modernisme who
counted Picasso and Miró among
his friends (they came to Sitges to
summer at his house). The
museum houses his impressive
collection of paintings and
drawings bequeathed on his death
to the town, including his own,
along with major works by
Picasso and El Greco.

MUSEU MARICEL

See p.100.

ESGLÉSIA DE SANT BARTOMEU I TECLA

See p.99.

Out to Lunch

You'll be hard-pushed to eat cheaply in Sitges –
and in the summer, even the handful of bad
restaurants are full. Those on a tight budget
should avoid the seafront, where the hotels serve
hit-and-miss paella and pasta meals to the
Eurotrash crowd. For a Catalan *menú del dia*
around the €7 mark – probably the best deal in
town – try the relaxed **El Celler Vell** in the
heart of gayland. The **Sucré Salé** crêperie also
does good-value three-course lunch options. If
it's ten deep at the **Café de Montroig** – and,
chances are, it will be – try **Villa Lola**, a quaint
juice and coffee bar tucked around a bend the
Platja de la Ribera beachfront.

EL CELLER VELL

ⓘ C. Sant
Bonaventura 21
🕿 93 811 19 61
💲 🍴

SUCRÉ SALÉ

ⓘ C. San Pau 39
🕿 93 894 23 02
💲 🍴

VILLA LOLA

ⓘ Passeig de la
Ribera
🕿 No Phone
💲 🍴

Sitges: Eating Out

If your wallet can stretch to it, it's relatively easy to eat well in Sitges. The Old Town is chock full of restaurants – C. de Sant Pau has a particularly strong concentration – and in high season it's worth dropping into one that takes your fancy on your way to the beach to guarantee a table later in the day. Fish and seafood are, inevitably for a fishing town, dishes of the day, but there's plenty of interesting international cuisine and vegetarian options to be had, too.

Cream of the Cuisine

Ma Maison

C. Bonaire 28
93 894 60 54

A gay-run garden restaurant in the heart of gaytown that scores full marks for ambience alone. The setting is idyllic – a tree-lined courtyard with plenty of leafy boughs, it's the perfect spot for a long, lazy lunch in the shade during a scorching summer afternoon. There's a select number of tables, mostly set for four, but romantic couples can be accommodated somewhere more snug. That it's impossibly pretty doesn't distract from the quality of the French-influenced modern European menu, which is impeccable. Deservingly, a much-loved gay fixture, popular with men and women.

The following price guides have been used for eating out and indicate the price for a main course:

= cheap = under €8

= moderate = €8–€17

= expensive = €17+

Can Pagès

ⓘ C. San Pere 24–26
☎ 93 894 11 95

One of the favourite eating options in Sitges has a renowned dynasty of chefs behind it. The Ramos family have long been offering typical Catalan seaside fare in rhyme with the season. Set back from the seafront, the interior is rustic in style, and there's a popular terrace that opens for the hot summer months. Fish fans will be happy with the inventive seafood stews, while there's a greater emphasis than most other restaurants in town on red meat, too. It's got that particular market cornered – the barbecue grill is the stuff of local legend.

Al Fresco

ⓘ C. Pau Barrabeitg 4
☎ 93 894 06 00

Foodies rate this among the best restaurants Sitges has to offer – and its menu is by no stretch typical of the town. Though there are regional influences (especially on the fish side), the menu is a globetrotting affair, borrowing heavily from the Middle East and the Pacific Rim as much as around the Mediterranean coast. This arty, off-the-wall backstreet bistro is the only place in town serving kangaroo.

Seafood snack in Sitges

SUCRÉ SALÉ
ⓘ C. San Pau 39
☎ 93 894 23 02

Busy garden restaurant with a menu of 'crêpes and things' that's light and varied. Besides the inventive pancake menu (not an especially Catalan speciality, but it keeps north Europeans happy), there are salads and chilled soups – perfect for the summer palate, and plenty for the healthy eater, too. All served in a delightful outdoor setting, or romantically low-lit indoors.

FLAMBOYANT
ⓘ C. Pau Barrabeitg 16
☎ 93 894 58 11

A spacious gay-run garden restaurant whose outdoor patio is dressed with towering purple flora and has a riotous party-party atmosphere, aided by the super-friendly staff. It'll be one of the most expensive meals you have during your stay, but the juicy steaks are worth splashing out on.

MONTY'S
ⓘ Passeig de la Ribera

Great little Italian with cheapo pasta

Best of the Rest

dishes and top-notch vegetarian options – perhaps the largest selection in town. Inevitably perhaps, it's very popular with lesbians.

GABRIEL
ℹ️ C. Sant Gaudenci 9
📞 93 894 30 46
🏳️‍🌈 🍽️

Intimate, gay-run French bistro – the calling card features a skin-headed sailor wielding his catch of the day. There's à la carte, but also a dinner buffet worth picking over.

CAFÉ DE MONTROIG
ℹ️ C. Marqués de Montroig 🏳️‍🌈 🍽️

Though not officially gay, it's hard to tell at this landmark café on the Montroig 'gauntlet' where the flirting reaches outrageous levels. Airy and continental, it does great cocktails as well as foamy coffees, in case you ever make it through the crowds to the bar or get to order at a hard-fought-over table.

LA SANTA MARÍA
ℹ️ Passeig Marítim 52
📞 93 894 09 99 🏳️‍🌈 🍽️

Occupying the most privileged location on the beachfront, this hotel-restaurant's terrace is one of the most elegant spots in town to be served *paellas* and *mariscos*. The faded glamour about the place – down to the retro plasticky menus – appears to appeal to the upmarket international clientele who've come fresh from the beach.

EL XALET
ℹ️ C. Illa de Cuba 35
📞 93 811 00 70
🏳️‍🌈 🍽️

Fine dining in the luxuriant gardens of a perfectly preserved Modernista house with tables set up – here's the twist – next to an inviting swimming pool. Expect a warm welcome from the owners, a relaxed atmosphere, and a good-value set menu.

Sitges: Out on the Town

Sitges has been a gay magnet since the 1960s, when it first began pulling in Spain's same-sex artist couples who were drawn to it by its historical links with the avant-garde and alternative lifestyles. Today, it vies with Ibiza for the title of Europe's most popular homo resort. While smaller – its 20,000 population swells to 80,000 in summer, thanks largely to an influx of gays – it is considerably more cosmopolitan than its brasher Balearic rival.

Its growing reputation in gay circles has happily resulted in a significant leap in the number of gay women visitors in recent years. Fittingly, there are whispers of a substantial slew of planned lesbian venues – at the moment, women have 'invited guest' status in many of the men's bars. Ask around for details of new openings. If the tourist information office is clueless, the staff at Hotel Liberty – which hosts its own lesbian Sunday nighter which is open to the public – will sort you out. At the height of the season, chances are you'll be turned away from a club or two. But don't worry – and don't try phoning ahead to check, there's no point. Just head around the corner to the next.

My Top Clubs

Trailer

 C. Angel Vidal 36 ❉ Daily 12am–6am

The legendary gay venue – this is Sitges's answer to Manumission – that's always packed with hot and sweaty bodies dancing well into the morning. Famed for its raucous Wednesday and Sunday night foam parties, plenty of revellers have reported difficulty getting the, er, watermarks out of their clubbing gear. Better check your clothes in, strip down to your under- or swimwear and get slippy with all the boys. Drinks are more pricey than at other venues, but you're guaranteed a night you won't forget.

Mediterraneo

ℹ️ C. Sant Bonaventura 16
🕐 Daily 10pm–3.30am

One of the most popular and relaxed places for a boogie, this is where most of Sitges ends up after a night's boozing. The club doesn't get busy until about 1am, when it fills to the brim. It looks small from the outside but it's split over two floors, with a pleasant chill-out gallery decorated with real palm trees – cool! Musically, expect an unpretentious, pumping mix of the latest handbag dance sounds – hands-aloft diva vocal tracks in both English and Spanish rule the roost here.

Parrot's Pub

ℹ️ Plaça de l'Industria
🕐 Daily from 5pm

The terrace opens early to catch the crowds coming in from the beach, and is a good place for early evening cocktails. Friendly and welcoming, Parrot's is popular with a relaxed mix of gay men, lesbians and their mates – basically, anyone who's under starter's orders

XXL

ℹ️ C. Joan Tarrida Ferratges 7
🕐 Daily 11pm–3.30am

One of the few places that stays open all year around, XXL is a well-established bar-cum-club that caters for all shapes and sizes – even regular, trim guys. The difference is that the music – and the scene – is heavier than most. Go for a spin around on the dance floor, or get drawn in by the X-rated vids playing all about the place. On Tuesday nights, it's time to strip off for the underwear parties. XXL is unpretentious fun, with friendly bar staff who go out of their way to make single travellers feel welcome. Not that you'll be single here for long.

So much to do

Who's a pretty boy?

for a night out in town. It's an unwritten local bylaw that the first drink of the night has to be in Parrot's. It's also worth popping in to pick up a copy of the free Sitges gay map and local listings rags. Essential.

Maripili

C. Joan Tarrida 14
Daily 12pm–3am

This is the centre of the women's scene in Sitges – the sole women-only joint. A friendly terrace café by day, it opens at midday and soon fills with chilled-out dykes from all over the world chatting about the previous night's conquests, while banishing hangovers with generous portions of hearty finger food. Once the sun's going down, and you've downed too much cappuccino and have watched the world go by (back to their hotels to tidy themselves up for another night out), the vibe shifts up a gear, becoming pre-clubby. It's worth popping back to pick up a flyer or two for the lesbian-approved gay clubs – and to check who's expected to show their face on the scene that night…

Best of the Rest

SEVEN

ⓘ C. Nou 5
🕐 Daily 10pm–3am

A buzzing bar, popular with early worms as well as the various local ex-pats who prop it up until the cavalry arrive later. *El siete* is one of the first to get busy – and when it does, you can't move. Enjoy a pre-dinner cocktail and watch the crowds pour in.

BAR AZUL

ⓘ C.ant Bonaventura 10
🕐 Daily 9pm–3am

This cabaret bar is not blue, as the name suggests, but bright orange. The name might have more to do with the blue movies it shows, as the sound system disconcertingly plays songs from the shows. There's a happy hour from 10pm to midnight in the summer months (April–October).

EL HORNO

ⓘ C. Joan Tarrida 6
📞 93 894 09 09
🕐 Daily 5.30pm–3.30am

Just round the corner from Parrot's, and popular with the leather and denim crowd. Has a video room and backroom upstairs that hosts underwear parties on

Organic club

Tuesdays and Thursdays. Happy hour until 7pm.

THE B-SIDE BAR

ⓘ C. Sant Gaudeneci 7
🕐 Daily 6pm–3am

Men-only bar, with darkroom and videos. Open all year round (closed Mondays October–June).

PIM'S MUSIC BAR

ⓘ C. Sant Bonaventura, 37

Want to hear your favourite showtunes lovingly recreated by the resident pianist? There's always a clutch of homo aficionados ready with their requests, preparing to weep into their whiskies at the opening bar of a Cole Porter classic or Hoagy Carmichael standard. A plush and intimate space, this is great place to unwind with a partner after a romantic meal.

BOURBON'S

ⓘ C. San Buenaventura 13
📞 93 892 33 47
🕐 Daily 10.30pm–3.30am

Discothèque ad – Sitges style

One for lovers of the dark – and a poseur's paradise. There are mirrors everywhere, even in the toilets, which reflect your full frontal around the gents. Get a few drinks down, then hit the dance floor or fumble your way around the darkroom until the lights come up.

EL CANDIL
ⓘ C. Carreta 9
☾ Daily 10pm–3am

Familiar combination of dance floor, darkroom and video screens. A good mix of music keeps this bar busy and racked with talent.

BAR COMODIN
ⓘ C. Tacó 5
✉ 93 894 16 98
☾ 10pm–3am

Open every day except Tuesdays. Closed in November. As expected from the Tom of Finland flyers, you get an older crowd here. The Saturday-night drag shows are popular and worth the detour.

THE ORGANIC CLUB
ⓘ C. Bonaire 15
✉ 93 894 22 30
☾ Daily 2am–6am

There's the latest sounds on a Friday and Saturday, and theme nights the rest of the week. Sunday's dance party is a step-back-in-time thrash with trash from the 70s onwards, and is always full with a lively, fun-loving crowd. On Tuesdays, Organic hosts a night at L'Alàntida, the open-air disco near the gay nudist beach. Check local press for details.

Out of Town

So you've partied in Barcelona and sunbathed in Sitges – what else does Catalunya offer the lesbian or gay traveller? Within a couple of hours of Barcelona there's Salvador Dalí's surrealist museum in Figueres; Cadaqués, the seaside village which inspired many of Picasso's greatest Cubist works; the mountain top monastery in Montserrat; the vineyard of Penedès… and even more sandy beaches by the bucket-load along the Costa Brava. The more adventurous might consider heading to Andorra, to the Pyrenees for skiing, to Valencia – or perhaps even to Ibiza, via the 9-hour ferry journey from the port (*see pp.135–136*).

Figueres

This windy inland town to the north of Barcelona was made famous by Salvador Dalí, who was born here in 1904 and died a recluse near the same spot in 1989. His museum is the main attraction, with exhibits as eyebrow-raising as the oddball's trademark pitchfork moustache. The surreal sights at the Teatre-Museu Dalí include a coin-operated Cadillac that rinses its interior with water; Dalí's rampart-like residence, Torre Galatea, topped with giant egg sculptures; and the Casa Mae West. The centrepiece is the artist's tomb, a wickedly macabre coffin fitted with a periscope that keeps watch over visitors. Figueres is also an increasingly popular base for a fabulous and mysterious lesbian community. You'll spot the ladies in wraparound sunglasses in the town's myriad cafés.

TEATRE-MUSEU DALÍ

ℹ️ Plaça Gala-Salvador Dalí 5
Figueres

📞 972 67 75 00

www.salvadordali.org

☼ July–Sept: Tues–Sun 9am–7.45pm;
Oct–June: Tues–Sun 10.30am–5.45pm

🎟️ €9

OFICINA DE TURISME DE FIGUERES

ℹ️ Plaça del Sol 📞 972 50 31 55
🚗 By car: A7 or N11 to Figueres (120kms from Barcelona) By train: RENFE from Sants or Passeig de Gràcia (2 hrs), departures every hour By bus: Several departures daily with Barcelona Bus (93 232 04 59) from Estació del Nord (metro: Arc de Triomf). Journey time 2–3 hours

Montserrat

Overlooking the river Llobregat 50 kilometres northwest of Barcelona is Montserrat, the 'serrated mountain' made from pillars of ragged rock that's so unworldly its knife-edged form looks like giant sculpture rather than anything geological. The shadow cast by its tallest peak – some 1,236m high – is said to have influenced Gaudí's design for the Sagrada Família. Arrive by train at the nearby station and you can take a cable car to the Gothic monastery halfway up. Founded in 1025, its wooden statue of La Moreneta, the Black Virgin, inside the basilica has been the focus of Christian pilgrimages for centuries. Time a visit right and you'll catch a performance from the Escolanía, a boys' choir founded in the 13th century, one of Europe's oldest, which is rarely heard beyond the monastery walls (1pm and 7.10pm, Mon–Sat). While there are plenty of cliff walks to be enjoyed – and the sights across the valley are miraculous – mountain-climbing is also possible. Call the tourist office for more details.

MONESTIR DE MONTSERRAT

ⓘ Plaça de Santa Maria   Montserrat

OFICINA DE TURISME DE MONTSERRAT

ⓘ Plaça de la Creu   Montserrat

☏ 93 877 77 77

www.abadiamontserrat.net

🚗 By car: C58 to Montserrat exit, then 7km mountain road to monastery

By train: FGC train from Plaça d'Espanya to Montserrat-Aeri station (up to 18 times daily), where you can get the cable car

Montserrat monument

Glorious Girona

across.  Ask for all-inclusive ticket (€16.90)

By bus: a Julià-Via bus leaves Sants bus station daily at 9am (earlier in summer), returning to Barcelona at 5pm. Journey time 75 mins.

Girona

Historically a tug-of-love between the Jews, Christians and Muslims, this well-preserved medieval hilltop town that is the largest in northern Catalunya is the undeniable jewel of the Costa Brava (not difficult, perhaps). At street level, it's a maze of steep stairs, narrow alleys and passageways worth exploring on foot. Must-sees include the colossal cathedral, a benchmark of Catalan Gothic that also has the world's largest nave (architects said it would never hold), 12th-century Arab baths *Banys Àrabs*, and the Pont de la Peixateries, an iron bridge built over the river Onyar by Eiffel (he of Parisian tower fame).

By car: A7 or N11 to Girona exit. 75kms
By train: RENFE from Sants or Passeig de Gràcia (1hr 15mins). Hourly 6am–9.15pm
By bus: Barcelona Bus, 3–7 daily, from Estació del Nord

OFICINA DE TURISME DE GIRONA

Rambla Llibertat 1
972 22 65 75

Tarragona

Declared a UNESCO world heritage site in 2000, this seaside city is one of Spain's oldest. It was the site of a military camp dating from the 3rd century BC that became the capital of Roman Iberia. Unsurprisingly, the sights within the old walled centre err on the imperial side: there's an ancient amphitheatre where many a gladiator met his end, and the remains of the vaulted circus (Circ Romà) once used for high-speed chariot racing. Thrillseekers today should head out of town to the new Universal Studios attraction, Port Aventura, for white-knuckle rides. There's also a magnificent Gothic cathedral, while nature lovers should not miss a boat trip around the wetlands of the nearby Ebre delta, which is a haven for 300 species of birds (and especially popular with flamingos).

AMFITEATRE ROMÀ
ⓘ Parc del Miracle ☎ 977 24 25 79

CIRC ROMÀ
☎ 977 24 19 52 🚇 Rambla Vella

PORT AVENTURA
ⓘ Apartado 90, Villa-Sec, Tarragona
☎ 902 20 22 20 www.portaventura.es/
☀ Mar–Nov 10am–midnight; June–Sept 10am–8pm 💳 One-day pass: adults €18, children €13. Two-day pass: adults €26, children €21. Three-day pass: adults €35, children €27

DELTA DE L'EBRE
ⓘ Information: 977 74 01 00 🚇 By car: A2, then either A7 via Vilafranca, or toll-free N340 (Molins de Rei exit). 100kms from Barcelona By train: RENFE from Sants or Passeig de Gràcia. Hourly departures 6am–9.30pm. 1hr–1hr 30mins By bus: Nine buses from Barcelona Nord on weekdays, just two at weekends. Takes 1hr 30 mins

OFICINA DE TURISME DE TARRAGONA
ⓘ C. Fortuny 4 ☎ 977 23 34 15

Cadaqués

Upmarket and a bolt hole for intellectuals, Cadaqués is to early 20th-century modern art what Giverny is to Impressionism. This whitewashed Costa Brava village with its bays, coves and isolated crags along the Cap de Creus peninsula moved Dalí (who had a house here) to speak of its 'grandiose geographic delirium' and entice his set, including Picasso, to paint here, too. See the fruits of their labours at the Museu de Cadaqués. Today, it retains its reputation as a suntrap for the rich holidaying Barcelona elite, and is perfect for wandering, for strolls along the pretty pebble beaches, and for eating in pricey but impeccable seafood restaurants.

MUSEU DE CADAQUÉS
ⓘ C. de Narcís Monturiol ☎ 972 25 88 77
🚇 By car: A7 to exit 4, then C260 to Cadaqués (2hrs) By bus: between two and five SAFRA buses (972 25 87 13) leave Estacio del Nord every day; Barcelona buses offer two services a day. Journey times 2hrs 15 mins

OFICINA DE TURISME DE CADAQUÉS
ⓘ C. del Cotxe 2 ☎ 972 25 83 15

Cadaqués, whitewashed Costa Brava village

Vilafranca de Penedès

The Penedès brand is now a familiar sight in bottle shops around the world, with this increasingly regarded wine-growing region, whose monks have been producing since the 11th century, known especially for its Cava (sparkling Catalan white) (*see p.77*) and various robust reds – as well as the occasional cheeky riesling. Visitors are welcome at many of the sprawling vineyards in the area (it's so large you're better off exploring in a car), while the Gothic palace in the town of Vilafranca de Penedès houses the impressive Museu del Vi. The small entrance fee includes a tasting. The largest and most important winemaker in the area, Miguel Torres, offers free tours and tastings at his vineyard (by appointment only).

MUSEU DEL VI

ℹ️ Palau Reial ☎ 93 890 05 82
🕐 Tues–Sat 10am–2pm, 4pm–7pm; Sundays and festival days 10am–2pm; closed Monday 🎫 €3

TORRES VINEYARD

ℹ️ Fina El Maset, Pacs del Penedès
☎ 93 817 74 87 www.torres.es
🕐 6am–10pm 🚇 By car: A2, then A7 to Vilafranca. 55kms from Barcelona
By train: RENFE to Vilafranca from Sants or Plaça Catalunya (45mins), departures every hour

OFICINA DE TURISME DE VILAFRANCA DE PENEDÈS

ℹ️ C. Cort 14 ☎ 93 892 03 58

The guides are free in selected gay bars, or by calling **THT Direct** on **0845 12 21 200** or email your postal address to **info@tht.org.uk**

Pam says ...

"Condoms? Buy BEFORE you fly"

Checking In

There's no such thing as low season in Barcelona – the city is always crammed with tourists. And at the height of summer, there's never quite enough accommodation to go round, hence the new arrivals snuggled up on the beach or checking into Sauna Casanova (*see p.97*) for the night. But if you book in advance, there are plenty of decent rooms going cheap.

Gay couples rarely confront problems in hotel receptions. But if you are booking into a straight hotel, before you arrive fax them you and your partner's names, confirming that you want a *cama doble* (double bed), just so there's no confusion.

At the lowest end of the market are the greatest bargains. And we're not talking flea-ridden backpackers' hostels, but *hostals*. A typically Spanish invention, *hostals* are usually clean, friendly and basically furnished townhouse apartments. Showers and bathrooms are often shared, though more upmarket operations will have en-suite options. They're a great way to keep costs down; get on with the owners and you've got a friend, tour guide and concierge to help with ticket bookings and restaurant recommendations. The downside is that they are often housed in old buildings, with thin walls and uncarpeted floors, so things can get noisy. Light sleepers might need a set of earplugs – but that's a small price to pay (cash only, of course).

Although it's worth having somewhere to stay in Barcelona before you arrive, those stuck for a place should make their first stop-off the tourist information centre on Plaça de Catalunya (*see pp.136–137*), which, for a small fee, will find you a room from a daily updated list of available accommodation.

Hotel Arts Barcelona

ⓘ C. Marina 19–21

☎ 93 221 10 00   Fax 93 221 10 70

www.ritzcarlton.com/hotels/barcelona

Ⓜ Ciutadella-Vila Olimpica 🏳️‍🌈 ❶

Barcelona's ritziest hotel is a landmark on its shoreline. At 44 storeys high, it is also the tallest building in Spain.

It's a popular choice with visiting dignitaries and celebrities – it was here that performers at the 2002 MTV Music Awards were put up in abject luxury – but it's also the perfect bolt hole for a gay stay.

Each of the luxurious rooms – 482 in total – has breathtaking panoramic views of the city and the sea, and it's a short walk from the Ramblas and the gay nudist beach Mar Bella. Great for a sightseeing city break or a dirty weekend.

The marble bathrooms have powerful walk-in power showers, there's a pillow menu and the offer of a butler-drawn bath. Before checking out, make sure you sweep up the freebie Bulgari toiletries. Pure indulgence!

Technophiles will love it, too. There's a Bang and Olufsen CD hifi, satellite TV and video in every room. When you've mastered those remote controls, there's always the electronically controlled blinds and light switches to play with…

As you'd expect, there's also an amazing gym – often seething with get-up-and-go execs – and a blissful beachfront pool for the less active.

If you've got the cash to splash, this is the place to stay.

The following price guides have been used for accommodation, per room per night

❶ = €10–€50

❷ = €50–€150

❸ = over €150

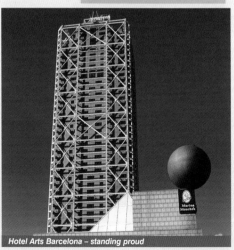

Hotel Arts Barcelona – standing proud

Hotel Claris

ℹ️ Pau Claris 150   📞 93 487 6262
Fax 93 215 7970 www.slh.com/claris
Ⓜ️ Passeig de Gràcia
🌈 ③

Bang in the heart of the Eixample, this is one of the most style-conscious hotels in the city. Scoring high in the chi-chi stakes – it's a former 19th-century palace, renovated with glass and gold, and just off the designer shopping drag, Passeig de Gràcia – it's also a tantrum's throw from the gay bars of the Gaixample and the lesbian hangouts in Gràcia. Rooms are decked out in dark wood and plush drapes in a riot of bold, continental purples, reds and oranges (very Catalan). Each has its own entry salon, complete with TV and mini-bar. The bathrooms have a shell-shaped bath big enough for two.

It's the perfect hideout for homos from home.

Hostal Qué Tal

ℹ️ C. Mallorca 290 (corner with C Bruc)
📞 93 459 23 66
www.quetalbarcelona.com
Ⓜ️ Passeig de Gràcia
🌈 ① Cash only

This long-standing favourite with gay travellers on tight budgets has a loyal following. Now it's so popular (admittedly, mostly with men, but women are made welcome) you have to book well in advance to secure a vacancy. And it's easy to see why. A converted Eixample townhouse with 14 rooms – and ever-expanding into neighbouring blocks – its rooms are clean, colourfully decorated in pastels, and deliciously cool in the sweaty summer months, when it's at its busiest.

Cheap and basic, Hostal Qué Tal (How Are You) has everything the low-rent traveller needs. Standard doubles come with a sink, wardrobe and a comfy bed, though there's also a choice of doubles with en-suite bathroom. A few rooms can sleep three and four persons – ideal for when sharing with friends. The shower rooms are kept immaculate by staff and guests alike. The prices speak for themselves, starting at €39 for a single with shared bath, €58 for a double with shared bath, and €74 for a double with own bath.

The staff are very friendly and discreet, speak first-rate English, and will happily keep you in mineral water and offer you freshly percolated coffee at any time of the day or night. They'll also advise you about where to go on the local scenes; the *hostal* is handy for both the gay and lesbian villages, pitched between the Gaixample and Gràcia. It's also within staggering distance from three of Barcelona's most popular men-only hangouts, New Chaps, Martins and the Eagle (so it gets the clone vote), as well as opposite Barcelona's hip LA Fitness gym. What more could you want?

Hostal Centro

ℹ️ C Balmes 83
☎ 649 550 238
info@absolutcentro.com
Ⓜ Passeig de Gràcia, Universitat
💳 💰 1️⃣
Cash only

This small and basic gay *hostal* prides itself on offering the cheapest 20 gay beds in Barcelona. With room rates starting at €35 a night (up to €75 for doubles), you'd expect to be a lot less central. But Centro is true to its name, with a great location in the heart of the Gaixample.

Run by the inscrutable owner, Jordi, it's a great option for gay couples, offering roomy doubles and pokier singles. (Guests on the pull inevitably turn a blind eye to the makeshift signs stating 'no visitors'.)

Hostal Centro is no beauty. It's furnished in a ramshackle style, with antique dressers plonked next to a flatpacked wardrobe that's in need of repair. The walls are thin, the corridors echoey, and rooms overlooking the main street rattle in the early hours with the last metro. (Try for the back room, which sleeps four and has its own belvedere balcony and minibar.) But ask anyone who's been to Barcelona before – you don't come to sleep. This is a fine option if you're just looking to close your eyes for a few hours before the party starts all over again…

Barcelona Rooms

ℹ️ C Comte d'Urgell 63
☎ 93 451 60 12, 629 159 759 (mob)
www.come.to/barcelonarooms
Ⓜ Urgell
💳 💰 1️⃣
Cash only

Barcelona Rooms is neither a hotel, a hostel, nor a *hostal*. Instead, it's a unique take on the guesthouse: gay-run, with 10 rooms done in modern décor, shared kitchen and TV lounge, and a convivial co-op feel.

There are his and hers shower rooms (it's as much for gay girls as for gay boys), a drinking fountain, and access to an iron (a rarity in most budget accommodation).

The shared kitchen is equipped with fridge, cooker, microwave and juicer – so you can shave costs off by self-catering. Though it's not a B&B, breakfast cereals are provided free. There's also a dining room for civilised 'house' get-togethers, which is also where newcomers are welcomed on their arrival with a glass of champagne.

Without doubt, this is the friendliest gay place to stay in Barcelona. Owners Pet and Sergi go out of their way to make all-comers welcome. They'll take you out for evening meals in the local tapas bar, and will happily escort you on a pub crawl until dawn, if so desired. And as if that wasn't enough, they'll also arrange massages for you with the live-in physiologist.

Located on a corner of the Gaixample, it's also handy for the airport: the A1 shuttle bus drops off and picks up right outside (ask the driver for Gran Via Urgell).

Accommodation Outlet

🌀 +44 (0)20 7287 4244
Fax +44 (0)20 7734 7217
www.outlet4holidays.com
🐸 ②-③

For less than the cost of a hotel, you could be spending your holiday in a designer pad of your own. London's gay accommodation experts, Outlet, offer short-let serviced apartments in Barcelona and Sitges (as well as Ibiza, London and San Francisco, too) for the gay traveller who prefers home comforts to hotels. Whether looking for somewhere to stay on your own, or for a party of eight or more friends, there'll be something on Outlet's books to suit.

Specialising in designer flats fit for style queens, their portfolio of privately-owned properties is ever growing, with apartments in Barcelona's Eixample, Barri Gòtic and around Arc de Triomf, as well as dotted around the narrow streets of Sitges's old town.

You're guaranteed a homely space full of decent crockery and glass-ware, a fridge, cooker, microwave – and extras like a satellite TV, DVD player and music system (bring your favourite compilations for a pre-clubbing warm-up).

Some of Outlet's swankier apartments go the extra kilometre, decked out with top-of-the-range Smeg kitchens, leather sofas, and – in one instance – a fantastic stone bath sunken into a polished concrete floor.

Check out the website to see what's on offer. It couldn't be more user-friendly. A definite hit.

Beauty and the Beach

ℹ️ Passeig Taulat 136 (5c)
🌀 93 266 05 62
www.beautyandthebeach.net
🚇 Poble Nou, bus 41 🐸 ②

If you're coming to Barcelona for a beach holiday, there's no better gay place to stay than this small and friendly bed and breakfast a few minutes' walk from the gay nudist strip, Mar Bella. And it's just a short

Beautiful B&B

bus hop to the Old City and La Rambla.

The three guest rooms at the top of a low-rise apartment block are plushly decorated in a contemporary palette, each with super-comfy queen-sized beds. The B&B is also fully air-conditioned – a definite boon during a scorching summer night. There's a TV lounge for quiet evenings in, and a hifi wired into the bathroom so you can get in the mood for a night out while plucking your eyebrows. All guests can check their emails and surf the web using wide-band internet access. And if you give advance warning, your hosts – a charming gay couple, José Marìa and Matt – will even cook for you. Blissful.

Centre of gay Sitges – Hotel Liberty

Hotel Liberty, Sitges

Illa de Cuba 45, Sitges 93 811 0872 www.hotel-liberty-sitges.com
RENFE train: Sitges

Stepping out of Sitges station, the rainbow-striped sign outside Hotel Liberty is the first indication that you've arrived in a gay wonderland. And this is the must-stay place for gay boys and girls in town – though even non-guests are welcome to stop off and pick up Sitges maps and listings guides from reception.

A painstakingly renovated turn-of-the-century townhouse over five floors, its 12 high-ceilinged rooms match period stylings with modern conveniences and comforts. Each guestroom is air-conditioned (though the stone floor helps keep things cool, too), and comes with satellite TV, minibar, phone and stereo system. Those facing the main road are triple-glazed – no chance of being woken by tipsy revellers staggering past – while those overlooking the gardens and pretty conservatory (where breakfast is served leisurely till midday) come with their own balconies and en suites.

The bar, with its relaxed, colonial feel, has a life of its own, hosting numerous local gay drinks parties, including a wildly popular girls' night. Located near the beach, bars and shops, Hotel Liberty is a gay idyll, and the multilingual staff work tirelessly to ensure a memorable stay.

Romantic by name...

AC DIPLOMATIC
ⓘ C. Pau Claris, 122
🚇 93 272 38 10
Fax 93 272 38 11
www.ac-hoteles.com
🚇 Passeig de Gràcia
💲💲 ③

One of Barcelona's
leading four-star
hotels, pitched
primarily at business
guests. But the
proximity to Gaudí's
major works, the
luxury shops on the
Passeig de Gràcia,
and the nearby bars
and clubs of the
Gaixample make it a
nifty bolt hole for
moneyed gay couples,
too.

HOTEL ACTUAL
ⓘ C. Rosselló 238
(corner with Passeig de
Gràcia)
🚇 93 552 05 50
Fax 93 552 05 55
www.hotelactual.com
🚇 Passeig de Grácia
💲💲 ②

Popular with the
trendy suits who do
business up on the A.
Diagonal, it's also
well-situated for the
gay scene tourist, a
short stroll from the
Gaixample bars.
Recently given a
sprightly facelift,
rooms are small, but
heavy on style: a
boutique feel on
a budget.

HOTEL CALIFORNIA
ⓘ C. Rauric 14 (corner
with C. Fernando)
🚇 93 317 77 66
Fax 93 317 54 74
www.seker.es/hotel_california

Welcome to the Hotel California

Sleeping Around

CHECKING IN

 Liceu

Gay-friendly two-star in a decidedly ropey alley off the Barri Gòtic (centrally located, though). Forgive the slight shabbiness: the laid-back boho air is the main attraction.

HOSTAL BAIRES

C. Avinyó 37
Tel/fax 93 319 77 74
hostalbaires@terra.es
Jaume I, Drassanes

Gay *hostal* set in a 17th-century palace in the Barri Gòtic, just five minutes from the Ramblas.

HOTEL GAUDÍ

C. Nou de la Rambla 12
93 317 90 32
Fax 93 412 26 36
www.hotelgaudi.es
 Liceu

Just off La Rambla in the Raval district, this well-placed mid-range hotel's connection to Antonio Gaudí extends beyond just the name. There's a secret tunnel (closed to the public) linking it with his extraordinary mock medieval palace opposite, which was commissioned by his long-time patron Eusabe Güell. Take the Palau Güell tour for

the full story (*see p.34*). Much of the grandiose palatial feel has stuck, and the public areas show strong nods to Gaudí's dreamy handiwork.

HOSTAL LAUSANNE

A. Puerta del Angel, 24 Plaça Catalunya
93 302 11 39, no fax
Catalunya

Well located on Barcelona's high-street shopping precinct, this gay-run (though not exclusively gay) two-star *hostal* opposite the El Corte Inglés has clean, functional rooms, with a large TV lounge and snack machine. Popular with young groups of backpacking friends.

HOTEL ORIENTE

La Rambla 45–47
93 302 25 58

Fax 93 412 38 19
www.husa.es
Drassanes

Reconstructed from a former monastery in 1842, this undisputed gem of the Barri Gòtic is now something of a museum piece. But the whiff of faded glamour only adds to the allure: Maria Callas would stay during her performances at the nearby Liceu opera house, and Errol Flynn holed up here in his heyday to escape adoring fans.

Fraying at the edges, the rooms are plain and perhaps a little pricey for a mid-range hotel on the Rambla. Still, it's perfect for enjoying the nightlife of the Barri Gòtic and the trendy Born district.

Faded glamour at the Oriente

TEDDY'S HOUSE

ℹ C. Roger de Llúria 104
☎ 93 458 71 40
teddyshouse@terra.es
Ⓜ Jaume I
🗺 ❶

Small, bear-friendly gay *hostal* in the Eixample.

TONY'S AND ALEX PLACE

ℹ C. Provença (corner with C Enric Granados)
☎ 661 69 28 36 (mobile)
www.tony-alex.com
Ⓜ Liceu 🗺 ❶

Modern gay guesthouse in the heart of Barcelona, run by a young couple. The first-floor apartment has three doubles and one single room for rent, with communal living room, sun terrace and laundry facilities. The top-of-the-range extras include cable TV, ADSL-connected PC, video and hi-fi.

Sitges

ANTONIO'S

ℹ Passeig Vilanova 58
☎ 93 894 92 07
Fax 93 894 64 43
antonios_sitges@hotmail.com
🗺 ❷

Five attractive guestrooms – some with en suite – and just a few minutes' walk from the beach.

Open for the summer season only (May–October).

CALIPOLIS HOTEL

ℹ Passeig Marítim
☎ 93 894 15 00
Fax 93 894 07 64
www.hoteles-hesperia.es
🗺 ❷

A mixed four-star hotel, but popular with same-sex couples, as it faces the main gay beach. Check in for the queerest sea view in Sitges.

LA MASIA CASANOVA

ℹ Passatge Casanova 8
☎ 93 818 80 58
Ⓜ Canyelles 🗺 ❷

Slightly off the beaten track in nearby Canyelles and set against a formidable mountain backdrop, this converted (and recently renovated) farmhouse winery, some 11 kilometres out of town, is a luxury gay spot. There's a pool and bar, plus a great sauna, Jacuzzi and steam room. Minimum three days' stay.

HOTEL DE LA RENAIXENÇA

ℹ C. Illa de Cuba 13
☎ 93 894 83 75
Fax: 93 894 81 67
🗺 ❶

Mixed gay-straight hotel pitched at the budget pocket. Rooms are small but clean, though the talking point is the lively bar, which has become a trendy meeting point for locals.

HOTEL ROMÀNTIC

ℹ C. Sant Isidre, 33
☎ 93 894 83 75
Fax: 93 894 81 67
www.hotelromantic.com
🗺 ❷

Set in gorgeous ornamental gardens – complete with palms, vines and spouting fountains – the 55-room hotel occupies three 19th-century villas, and has retained its period charm. Perfect for lovers of outdoor dining is the garden restaurant, which, with its fantastic wine list and champagne cellar, is gourmet heaven.

The following price guides have been used for accommodation, per room per night
❶ = €10–€50   ❷ = €50–€150
❸ = over €150

Panorama of the Plaça d'Espanya

Check This Out

These pages cover everything you need to know about getting to Barcelona. They tell you what to do to stay healthy, how to make the most of your money, and advise you about sex in the city. Find out when it's hot, when the parties are, and how generally to stay out of trouble.

Getting There

BY AIR

FLYING FROM THE UK

Regular flights to Barcelona's El Prat de Llobregat airport (BCN) depart from all major international airports, including London's main three. It is a fiercely competitive route, with low prices to be had on most carriers. The flight time from London is 1hr 45mins.

The most comfortable option is British Airways (www.ba.com, 0845 773 3377), which offers an extensive direct schedule every day from London Heathrow and London Gatwick, Manchester, Birmingham and Glasgow airports. Thanks to price slashing in recent years, BA can be better value than 'budget' rivals, with single flights from £39 (plus tax) and return tickets for around £100. Iberia (www.iberia.com) also operates from various UK airports.

Of the numerous 'no frills' airlines travelling to Barcelona, the market leader is EasyJet (www.easyjet.com). The airline operates most flights from London

Luton, as well as London Gatwick, London Stansted, Liverpool, Glasgow, Bristol, Newcastle and East Midlands. BMIbaby (British Midland's budget airline, www.bmibaby.com) offers a 'no frills' service from East Midlands airport, and budget newcomer Jet2 (www.jet2.co.uk) flies from Leeds-Bradford.

The internet makes planning a trip to Barcelona simple. Try the following websites:

www.airfares.co.uk
www.cheapflights.co.uk
www.deckchair.com
www.dialflight.com
www.expedia.co.uk
www.flightbookers.com
www.opodo.co.uk
www.statravel.co.uk
www.thomascook.co.uk
www.travelocity.co.uk

Charter flight operators also fly to Barcelona from main and regional airports, with return flights starting at as little as £80. Check out the travel classifieds of *Time Out*

CHECK THIS OUT

and *Loot*, or Teletext, for more details.

FLYING FROM NORTH AMERICA

Delta Airlines (www.delta.com) flies direct to Barcelona three times a day from New York. Iberia also operates a daily overnight service from Miami. Air Canada, Delta, Iberia and American Airlines all fly via Madrid, and have extensive travel networks using partnership airlines via other European capitals. It may prove more economical to fly into London Heathrow and fly onwards with a British carrier. (*See p.133.*)

The prices for indirect flights from North America to Barcelona range from $350 to $1,000. Try the following sites:

www.airbrokers.com
www.statravel.com
www.travelcuts.com
www.travelocity.com

FLYING FROM AUSTRALIA AND NEW ZEALAND

There are no direct flights to Spain from Australia and New Zealand, though Qantas (www.qantas.com.au) flies from both countries with a series of stopovers (usually London Heathrow).

ARRIVING IN BARCELONA

Barcelona's El Prat de Llobregat airport (93 298 3838, www.barcelona-airport.com) is a convenient 13 kilometres (7 miles) south of the city. There are two main international terminals, A and B (C is for domestic routes). It is clean, orderly and with all the usual distractions: shop, cafés, tourist information offices (open 9am–5pm), cash machines and bureaux de change (open 7am–11pm). There are also left luggage lockers in Terminal B.

For up-to-the-minute information on flights to and from Barcelona, consult the airport website, www.barcelona-airport.com. The site also has weather forecasts – handy for last-minute packing adjustments.

GETTING FROM THE AIRPORT

AEROBUS

A simple way to get into the city centre, the A1 Aerobus leaves directly outside terminal buildings A and B every 15 minutes between 6am and midnight. It takes about half an hour to Plaça de Catalunya, with stop-offs at Plaça d'Espanya and Gran Via de les Corts Catalanes. Returning to the airport, it leaves Plaça de Catalunya along C d'Aragó (in the Gaixaimple), with pick-ups at Sants station and Plaça d'Espanya. The price is €3.30 one-way (*sencilla*) or €5.65 return (*ida y vuelta*). The Aerobus is wheelchair accessible. Two local buses, 105 and 106, serve both airport terminals from Plaça d'Espana. They take longer but cost only €1 each way, and run later; the last 106 leaves the airport at 3.20am. Heading to the airport, the last 106 leaves Plaça d'Espanya at 3.50am. There is also a nightbus (*nitbus*) service to the airport, route EN, which picks up from Plaça de Catalunya, Plaça d'Espanya, and along Gran Via de les Corts Catalanes.

RENFE TRAIN

The RENFE train takes 20 mins to Barcelona Sants, 25 mins to Plaça de Catalunya, 27 mins to Arc de Triomf, and 31 mins to El Clot-

Aragó. Trains operate every 30 mins between 6.13am and 11.40pm, and cost €2 one-way. Returning to the airport, the train stops at Plaça de Catalunya every 8 and 38 mins past the hour.

TAXI

Expect to part with between €12 and €25 for a metered cab from outside the two main terminals, depending on traffic and where in the city you want to go. Fares are higher (by 10–20 per cent) after 10pm, and at weekends, and there is a 80¢ surcharge for each piece of luggage put in the boot. There is usually an abundance of taxis waiting so you shouldn't require the services of the taxi touts operating inside the terminal building.

ARRIVING BY BUS

It is possible to travel from London to Barcelona by bus, though the 24-hour journey will deter all but the most nervous of flyers. Eurolines (www.eurolines.com) offers single tickets from around £80, with returns from £110, though restricted Apex returns may be as little as £60.

Bussing into Barcelona is a more likely mode of transport for those already travelling in mainland Spain or neighbouring countries. Most long-distance buses come into the modern Estació d'Autobuses Barcelona-Nord (C Al Del 80, 93 265 65 08), a five-minute walk from Arc de Triomf metro. Some services – including Eurolines – also stop at Sants station.

For those travelling on from Barcelona by bus, services are mostly operated out of Barcelona Nord – by Enatcar (93 245 88 56, www.enatcar.com) and its subsidiary, Alsa (902 422 242,

Tourist information

www.alsa.es). During busy periods, it is advisable to book a seat at least 24 hours in advance.

ARRIVING BY TRAIN

Barcelona's main international and domestic station is Sants Estació, some 3 kilometres from Plaça de Catalunya, or a short metro journey (on the green L3 line). Sants is large, well equipped and unthreatening. Spain's state-run rail service is RENFE (902 24 02 02, www.renfe.es). For local journeys, use coins and euro notes in the ticket machines (which have optional instructions in English). Otherwise, there are tellers who often speak rudimentary English.

Some French services terminate at the impressive and underused 1920s Estació de Franca, close to Barceloneta metro.

ARRIVING BY SEA

Those considering a trip to Barcelona following a holiday on the Balearic island of Ibiza should consider the naval option. The Umafisa ferry (971 31 02 01, www.umafisa.com) docks at (and departs from) the Moll de Barcelona quay at the end of Avinguda Parel.lel. There's a 9-hour overnight sailing every day except Sunday, and prices range from €45.43 for lounge seating, and from €54 to €155.80 for a cabin, depending on facilities and occupancy.

Transmediterranea (93 295 91 34/35, www.transmediterranea.es) operates regular services to and from Ibiza, with prices between €26.20 and €150.40. Both companies sail to Ibiza at night – but you can arrive in Barcelona from the island on a daytime sailing, perfect for topping up the tan.

ENTRY REQUIREMENTS

PASSPORTS AND VISAS

For trips of under three months, full passports are required by visitors from the UK, Ireland, Canada, USA, Australia and New Zealand. Citizens of the UK and Ireland planning to stay in Spain for more than this time need to obtain a residency permit (*permiso de residencia*) from the foreigners' office (*Oficina de Extranjeros*) at the Delegación del Gobierno (Avda Marques de Argentera 2, 93 482 05 60, metro Barceloneta, appointments 8am–3pm Mon–Fri). Non-EU nationals will need to obtain a visa in their own country prior to departure if they wish to stay for more than three months. As visa requirements frequently change, check with your Spanish Embassy if planning a long stay.

PEOPLE WITH HIV/AIDS

Spain has no specific restrictions on entry for people living with HIV/AIDS. Non-EU nationals applying for residency, work and student permits will be required to take a medical test. When travelling with anti-retroviral medication, ensure it is clearly labelled.

CUSTOMS

It is not usually necessary to make customs declarations if arriving from another EU country. You can bring in with you: 800 cigarettes or 400 cigarillos, 200 cigars or 1 kilo of loose tobacco, 10 litres of spirits (over 22 per cent alcohol), 20 litres of fortified wine or alcoholic drinks (under 22 per cent alcohol), plus 90 litres of wine and 110 litres of beer. Be warned that if you are carrying quantities this high, you could be asked to explain how it is all for personal use.

Non-EU residents can bring in 200 cigarettes or 100 cigarillos, 50 cigars or 250g of loose tobacco; plus one litre of spirits (over 22 per cent alcohol) or 2 litres of fortified wine or spirits under 22 per cent, plus 2 litres of wine and 50 grams of perfume. Non-EU residents can claim back VAT (*IVA*) for purchases of over €90 – enquire at the airport on arrival or in the store as you buy.

In the city

TOURIST INFORMATION

Barcelona's well-staffed central tourist office on Plaça de Catalunya (906 30 12 82, www.barcelonaturisme.com) is

Hop on and get around town

open 9am–9pm daily. The English-speaking staff will supply you with free maps and information. You'll also find a hotel booking service (useful in an emergency, but you'll have to stand in very lengthy queues), bureau de change, souvenir shop and coin-operated internet access.

There are other tourist inform-ation offices in Sants station, open 8am–8pm (2pm closing at weekends in winter) and Plaça Jaume (10am–8pm, 10am–2pm weekends). In the summer, a mobile tourist information booth stands outside La Sagrada Família – look out for the red-jacketed information officers.

All tourist information offices are marked with a red sign with a white 'i' in the centre.

The city also offers a useful telephone information service, manned Mon–Sat, 9am–10pm. Dial 010 from any phone, and the operators will efficiently answer most queries you may have.

For those interested in exploring beyond Barcelona's city limits, there is a Turisme de Catalunya office in Palau Robert (Passeig de Gràcia 105, 93 238 40 00). Open 10am–7pm Mon–Sat, 10am–2pm Sunday.

ACCOMMODATION

Most hotels, hostels and guesthouses will display metropolitan attitudes towards same-sex couples. If at all worried, simply mention that you are gay when booking, but it shouldn't present a problem. Barcelona still has something of an accommodation crisis, so as a rule it is best to arrange somewhere to stay before arriving.

PUBLIC TRANSPORT

Barcelona is blessed with an efficient and integrated metro, train and bus network. The public transport

website, www.tmb.net. is extremely useful. Not only can you search for public transport options on an address, area and even landmark, you can also click your starting point on a map, enter your destination, and it will provide you with a detailed description of the best way to get there, with journey times and any additional walking directions – all in English and printable.

METRO

The Barcelona metro is fast, clean and easy to use. It consists of five lines, easily identified by number and colour. At interchange points the signs state the final destination for trains stopping at each platform. A single journey costs €1.05, but the best option is usually a T-10 carnet which costs €5.80. This allows you ten trips, each with a free interchange onto any RENFE or FGC train, metro or bus within 1 hour 15 mins of validation. The same ticket can be used by more than one person, so one card will allow you and a partner or friend to take five trips together. Pass the ticket back over the gates once the first person has gone through.

There are also cards offering unlimited travel for €4.40 to €17.30 for between one and five days, and €35.70 for a month (T-Mes). These prices are for zone 1, which covers anywhere you'd reasonably want to go in the city, apart from the airport.

Cards can be bought from machines and ticket offices inside stations, lottery shops, the ServiCaixa ticket centres (which also sell gig, theatre and cinema tickets) and newspaper kiosks, but not on buses. Many new machines take credit and debit cards, but will require a PIN number for security.

Metro travel

You will only require your ticket to enter a station; there are few exit barriers, but hold on to it; fail to show a ticket on demand and you could face a €40 fine.

The Metro runs 5am–midnight Mon–Thur, 5am–2am Friday and Saturday, 6am–midnight Sunday.

BUS

Most bus routes operate 5am–10.30pm, with buses passing every 10–15 mins. Services become less frequent later in the evening and on Sundays. Only single journeys (€1.05) can be purchased on the bus; for multi-journey tickets valid on the buses, see 'Metro'. If you have a ticket like a T-Mes, simply insert it into the validation machine behind the driver. To ensure a bus stops, you need to flag it down as you would a taxi. Board at the front and get off at the middle or rear.

NIGHTBUS

Nightbuses (*nitbuses*) run on 16 urban routes 10.30pm–4am. They operate every 20–30 mins and most pass through Plaça de Catalunya, which is also the terminus for several services to areas further from the centre. Nightbuses work on the same pricing and ticketing system as daytime buses.

TRAINS

If heading out of Barcelona city centre, there is an extensive train network. RENFE and the FGC (www.fgc.net) run suburban trains and services to surrounding towns. For Sitges, take the train from Sants station. Fares vary depending on zones.

Travelling to Madrid from Sants, allow six to nine hours and expect to pay between €30 and €45 for standard class (*turista*), and up to €58 for first class (*preferente*). The Trenhotel operates an overnight service, the 'Antonio Gaudí', to the capital (www.renfe.es/empresa/glineas/glineas_hotel.html); a high-speed rail link between the two cities is expected to open in 2004. A train to Valencia will take around five hours and cost between €29 and €33.50 turista.

TAXIS

Barcelona's taxis are yellow, black and plentiful – about 11,000 in total (most of them Skodas!). A taxi with an illuminated green light on the roof with a '*Lliure/Libre*' sign in the window is for hire. Hail it as you would in any other city. Taxi ranks are located at major bus and train stations and other locations throughout the city centre.

The minimum fare is €2, and you will be charged extra for luggage and waiting time. Drivers may not carry more than €15 change; not many accept card payments. You shouldn't have difficulty finding an available taxi, or call or book online:

Fono-Taxi: 93 300 11 00
Radio-Taxi: 93 225 00 00
Radio Taxi '033': 933 033 033
www.radiotaxi003.com (Spanish)
Servi-Taxi: 933 300 300
www.servitaxi.com (Spanish)
For disabled-adapted taxi. Call 93 481 1058 or 93 528 1111.

CAR HIRE

Hiring a car is a recommended option if travelling around Catalunya. Good public transport, bad parking and pleasant walking may put you off hiring if you are staying within the city. Drivers must be at least 21 years old (or up to 25 with some companies) and hold a valid driving licence. A credit card will be needed for the large deposit.

Europcar (www.europcar.com) has several depots across the city, at the airport, and in Sitges. Book in advance online. A compact car costs €300 for a week, or if you prefer racing through the Catalan countryside in style, convertibles start at €515.

EasyCar (www.easycar.com) has remarkably cheap car hire starting at €6 basic charge per day with depots at Sants station and Arc de Triomf in the centre.

In the heart of the Gaixample, try Avis (C Casanova 209, 93 209 95 33) and Atesa/National (C Muntaner 45, 93 298 34 33). Both also have offices at the airport.

EMBASSIES

Embassies and Consulates are listed in the phone book under Consolats/Consulados. If calling outside office hours, most have an emergency contact number.

AUSTRALIA

Gran Via Carlos III 98, Zona Alta (93 330 94 96, fax 93 411 09 04, www.embaustralia.es). Metro Maria Cristina or Les Corts. Buses 59, 70, 72. Open 10am–midday Mon–Fri. Closed August.

CANADA

C. Elisenda de Piños 10, Zona Alta (93 204 27 00, fax 933 204 27 01, www.canada.es.org). No metro, FGC train Reinda Elisenda. Buses 22, 64, 75. Open 10am–1pm Mon–Fri.

NEW ZEALAND

Travesera de Gràcia 64 (93 209 03 99, fax 93 202 0890). Metro Passeig de Gràcia. Buses 22, 24, 48. Open Sept–June 9am–2pm and 4pm–7pm. Phone to check reduced hours in August.

REPUBLIC OF IRELAND

Gran Via Carlos III 94, Zona Alta (93 491 50 21, fax 93 411 29 21). Metro Maria Cristina or Les Corts. Buses 59, 70, 72. Open 10am–1pm Mon–Fri.

UNITED KINGDOM

Avinguda Diagonal 477, Eixample (93 366 62 00, fax 93 366 62 21, www.ukinspain.com). Metro Hospital Clínic. Buses 6, 7, 15, 33, 34. Open end of Sept–mid-June 9.30am–1.30pm, 4–5pm Mon–Fri. Mid-June–mid-Sept 9am–2pm.

UNITED STATES

Passeig Reina Elisenda 23 (93 280 22 27, fax 93 205 52 06, www.embusa.es). No metro, FGC train Reina Elisenda. Buses 22, 64,

Travel Tips

Barcelona bound? Then check out these travellers' health tips.

IF YOU'RE ILL

British passport holders are entitled to free or reduced cost emergency medical care (including emergency HIV-related treatment). But you may have to pay then claim the money back. Using the E111 scheme will mean quicker access to this health care. Get the form from your post office (they must stamp it, too) and take it (and a photocopy) on holiday. One E111 form will cover multiple trips within Europe (you'll only need a new one if you change address). Without an E111 you may face charges. It covers tourists but not those studying or working in Spain.

The E111 only gets you basic treatment and is not an alternative to your own private insurance (which covers things the E111 scheme doesn't, like theft, lost luggage, etc.). Travellers wanting insurance that covers HIV-related problems can get details of firms offering that from THT Direct on 0845 12 21 200 (10am–10pm).

No vaccinations are needed for Spain.

For more on health care abroad check out *www.doh.gov.uk/traveladvice/treatment2.htm*

TRAVELLING WITH HIV MEDICATION

There are no travel restrictions for people with HIV visiting Spain as tourists. To avoid raising suspicions with Customs officials it's better to leave medication in its original packaging. A note from your doctor might be useful, explaining the drugs are for a 'chronic infection' (without mentioning HIV).

Suitcases can go missing so medicines are best carried in hand luggage.

CONDOMS

Don't rely on free condoms and lube being available in Spanish gay venues. Take enough of both away with you so you won't be caught unprepared.

CONTACT

For help with HIV or sexual health related issues in Barcelona the AIDS Information Line (900 21 22 22) has advice and information on local services from 9am–5.30pm Mon–Fri mid-Sept–May, 8am–3pm Mon–Fri June–mid-Sept.

Casal Lambda (C Verdaguer i Callis 10, Barri Gòtic 93 319 55 50, www.lambdaweb.org, metro Urquinaona, buses 17,19,40,45) is a cultural centre and meeting point for gays and lesbians. It is open 6–9pm Mon–Sat.

Terrence HiGGins Trust

75. Open 9am–12.30pm and 3pm–5pm Mon–Fri.

POLICE

In terms of police attitudes towards gays, Catalonia is the most advanced area of Spain, and Barcelona's police forces are renowned for their metropolitan-mindedness.

If a crime is committed against you, report the incident as soon as possible to the local police force, the *Guardia Urbana*. You should go to the nearest police station (*comisaria*). You will need to fill in an official statement form (*denuncia*) which will be required for any insurance claims. It will be available in English. The most central *comisaria* is located at La Rambla 43 (93 344 13 00, metro Liceu or Drassanes, buses 14, 38, 59 or 91). Open 24 hours, it often has English-speaking officers on duty. At 7am–midnight Sun–Thur and 7am–2am Fri and Sat, you can go to the Turisme-Atenció at the same address – this office specialises in assisting tourists, and is particularly helpful with filling out *denuncias*.

To be connected to the nearest *comisaria*, call the Policia Nacional on 93 290 30 00.

Copy your passport and travel documents and leave them in your hotel – they will help considerably if the originals are lost or stolen. By law, you should carry some form of official ID, such as an identity card or passport.

In an emergency, call the Policia Nacional on 091. For non-urgent matters, contact the Guardia Urbana on 192.

ATTITUDE TOWARDS GAY VISITORS

Gay men and lesbians are a crucial, visible part of Barcelona, so you should feel relaxed roaming the city. Attitudes become more conservative the further away from the city you travel, and you may find open signs of affection attract stares but rarely anything more threatening.

Remember, gay men in particular are often a target for petty, rather than hate, crime. Use common sense.

DRUGS

While drugs are widely available from scooter-riding sellers patrolling the streets of the Gaixample, all non-prescription drugs are illegal. Cannabis is widely, and often openly, used, but it is still illegal to possess or consume in public places. Though the law permits smoking in private, you can still be arrested for possession.

Police presence

CHECK THIS OUT

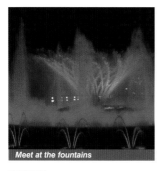
Meet at the fountains

SAFETY

Bag snatching and pickpocketing are common in Barcelona. It pays to take care along La Rambla, around the port and Barri Xinès at night, and in all crowded areas like the metro. Barcelonans party late so it's unlikely you'll ever be walking a main street alone at night. But if in doubt, take a taxi or nightbus. (*See pp.137–139.*)

Women should feel comfortable in most parts of the city. It is safe for women to walk in pairs in quiet areas at night, but single women should take a taxi.

HEALTH

Visitors to Barcelona can receive emergency medical treatment through the public health service – call 112 to be connected to an ambulance, or 061 direct. Several central hospitals, like the seafront Hospital del Mar, have casualty departments (*Urgéncies*). Phone 010 for information about your nearest hospital and medical practitioner.

EU nationals can get basic medical treatment for free with a valid E111 form. Non-EU nationals with private health insurance can receive state healthcare on a paying basis.

Don't expect gay bars and clubs to give away free condoms and lube. Most gay saunas – certainly those recommended in the *Working Out* section – hand out one condom on entry (though not always lube).

For travellers with HIV/AIDS, anti-retroviral medication comes under Spanish Social Security. To obtain extra supplies, a prescription is needed; some medications may have a different name and you would need to visit a doctor – therefore, it is advisable to bring enough medication for your stay.

The AIDS Information Line (900 21 22 22) has advice and information on local services from 9am–5.30pm Mon–Fri mid-Sept–May, 8am–3pm Mon–Fri June–mid-Sept.

GAY RESOURCES

Casal Lambda (C. Verdaguer i Callis 10, Barri Gòtic 93 319 55 50, www.lambdaweb.org, metro Urquinaona, buses 17,19,40,45) is a cultural centre and meeting point for gays and lesbians that has been supporting the local gay community and campaigning for gay rights since 1976. It is open 6–9pm Mon–Sat, often with social events at weekends. It is a good contact point for single travellers looking to be guided onto the local scene (their magazine *Lambda* has a useful listings section).

COMMUNICATION

TELEPHONES

Most payphones accept coins (minimum 2 cents), Telefónica phonecards and credit cards. A local call will cost about 15 cents, 50 cents to a mobile. Post offices, kiosks (*estancs*) and newsstands sell Telefónica phonecards.

Mobile phones (*móviles*) are now very popular in Barcelona. Rent a

Phone allows you to rent mobile phones for the duration of your stay. They have a branch in the Gaixample (C. Numància 212, 93 280 21 31, www.rphone.es), and also at the Maremàgnum shopping mall at Port Vell (93 225 81 06).

To make an international call, dial 00 then the country code and the local area code (removing the first 0 for the UK) and number. The country codes are:

Australia: 51
Canada: 1
New Zealand: 64
Republic of Ireland: 353
United Kingdom: 44
United States: 1

INTERNATIONAL OPERATOR ASSISTANCE

Dial 1008 for Europe and North Africa, 1005 for the rest of the world. Most operators speak English. For International Directory enquiries, dial 025.

TO CALL BARCELONA

Dial your country's exit code (eg. 00 in the UK) then 34 for Spain. All local numbers in Barcelona have nine digits – if you see one with seven, put 93 in front of it. For National Directory Enquiries, dial 025 – usually operators will speak only Spanish and Catalan.

EMERGENCY NUMBERS

For emergency services, dial 112. The operator will connect you to the police (policia), fire service (bomberos), or ambulance services (ambulancia), as requested. Alternatively, dial:
Ambulance/Ambulància: 061
Fire Service/Bombers/Bomberos: 080
Policia Nacional: 092 (first choice for a police emergency).

INTERNET

Internet centres and cafés can be found all over Barcelona. The best place is Ciberopcion (Gran Via de les Corts Catalanes 602, 93 412 73 08, www.ciberopcion.com), near the university. It has fast connection, English-speaking staff, access for 60 cents per 30 mins, plenty of terminals and a decent juice bar. Open 9am–1am Mon–Sat, 11am–1am Sun.

POST OFFICE

The main central post office, Correu Central (Plaça Antoni Lopez, 93 486 83 02, metro Jaume I or Barceloneta, buses 14, 17, 19, 36, 40, 45, 57, 59, 64, 157), is at the foot of the Barri Gòtic. Open 8.30am–9.30pm Mon–Sat, 9am–2pm Sun. Post boxes are yellow and marked Correos y Telégrafos. Collections are Monday to Friday only.

Barcelona is scattered with estancs/estancos, the traditional tobacco kiosks that also sell postage stamps, transport targetes and phonecards. They are marked with a brown and yellow sign and the word tabac or tabacos. Good for avoiding post office queues.

MONEY

Since 2002, Spain's official currency has been the euro. One euro (€) consists of 100 cents (¢), also referred to as centims in Catalan, centimes in Castillian. Euro notes come in denominations of 5, 10, 20, 50, 100, 200, and 500, with coins of 1 and 2 euros.

Banks (bancos) will change travellers' cheques and cash for a commission. They won't change personal cheques except those they have issued. Banks are normally open 8.30am–2pm Mon–Fri, and

CHECK THIS OUT

8.30am–1pm Sat Oct–April only. Savings banks (which offer the same exchange services as normal banks) are also open 4.30pm–7.45pm on Thursdays Oct–May.

Foreign Exchange offices (*cambios*) are generally open later – 7am–11pm in both terminals at the airport; 8.30am–9.30pm in Sants station, and 8.30am–10pm Mon–Fri, 9am–5.30pm Sat–Sun in Barcelona Nord bus station. Several *cambios* along La Rambla remain open until midnight, some as late as 3am (July–Sept only). Some *cambios* don't charge commission, but you'll find their rate is probably lower.

The most convenient option is using ATMs (*telebancos*), which are very common and have instructions in English. As they charge a minimum fee, it makes sense to withdraw larger amounts of cash.

In emergencies, the quickest way to have money wired is Western Union (Loterias Manuel Martin, La Rambla 41, 93 412 70 14, metro Liceu, buses 14, 38, 59, 91, open 9.30am–11pm Mon–Sat, 10am–midnight Sun).

In an emergency try the following numbers. All are open 24hrs and have English-speaking operators:
American Express: 902 37 56 37
Diners Club: 901 10 10 11
MasterCard: 900 97 12 31
Visa: 900 99 12 16.

TIPPING

Tips are appreciated but not always expected. In a restaurant, leave between five and ten per cent.

CREDIT CARD KEY
Amex = American Express
DC = Diners Club
M = MasterCard
V = Visa

Some also leave a small tip for bar staff, and it is normal to tip hotel porters, chambermaids, and toilet/restroom attendants. As a guide, tip a taxi driver five per cent of the fare, or more if they have been particularly helpful.

EATING OUT

Catalans eat late. Restaurants open around 1.30pm–4pm for lunch (the main meal), and for dinner 9pm–11.30pm. In between meals, take the edge off hunger with a pastry and hot chocolate in a *granja* bar.

Touristy restaurants have earlier opening hours. Cafés and café bars often open at 7am for breakfast and can stay open until past midnight. Bars tend to have a flurry from 7pm, but expect most to be quiet until at least 10.30pm, then lively until 3am. Clubs open around midnight and keep going – 7am–9am on Saturday and Sunday.

OPENING HOURS

Generally, shops are open 9/10am–1/2pm and 4.30/5pm–8/9pm, though many do not re-open in the afternoon on Saturdays. Many department stores and shopping centres stay open 10am–9pm Saturday, with some open on Sunday.

Museums follow shop hours but often reduce their hours in the winter months. Most close on Monday. Smaller museums can be reluctant to apply a regular timetable, so phone ahead.

ELECTRICITY

The standard current is 220V or 225AC. Australian, British, Irish and New Zealand visitors can use two-pin adaptor plugs, available in travel shops and airports (or Barcelonan department stores if you forget to bring one). For standard Canadian and US 110V appliances, a current transformer will also be needed. A few old buildings still use 125V. In cheaper hotels, check before plugging in your appliances.

CLIMATE

Barcelona has good weather all year round. July and August are very hot, though the sea breeze often prevents it getting too humid. May, June and early September have great warm and sunny weather. October to December is fresh, sometimes with downpours (often in the evening).

SCENE

The Barcelona gay scene is big all year round, with bars and clubs reaching their capacity in the summer months.

The gay scene in Sitges throbs between June and early October, while in the winter and spring it is a relaxed and sleepy seaside town; most gay bars and clubs are closed but there is still a visible gay presence, and February's Carnival is huge.

Media

GAY PRESS

Most gay and some cultural venues stock free gay publications like the A3 style freesheet *Shangay*, its pocket-sized spin-off, *Shanguide*, and the slightly worthier *Lambda* (www.lamdaweb.org). Trendy free monthly *Nois* (www.revistanois.com) has very useful scene maps. For sheer portability and clarity, you can't beat *Friends: The Gaymap*, available

Buy souvenirs with euros

individually in Barcelona and Sitges, and written in Spanish and English (www.friends.ag). Available in most city-centre kiosks is the gay men's monthly *Zero* (www.zeropress.com), which likes to hide its serious-minded content behind sexy-model coverstars. It also includes a handy pullout Spanish scene guide, *Guía Zero*.

GENERAL LISTINGS

Barcelona's ultimate listings guide is gay-inclusive *Guía del Ocio*, available at newsstands and kiosks (www.guidelociobcn.es). You may also be handed a free copy of *Barcelona@Mas* or *Metro* on the metro, both good for listings.

TV AND RADIO

Barcelona's TV is rarely worth staying in for. Radio stations in Barcelona are abundant, and Catalan is prominent. BBC World Service can be found on 15485 and 9195 KHz. Digital radio owners can also listen to Barcelona's gay radio station. See www.gaybarcelona.net for details.

Useful phrases

Listed first in Spanish, then Catalan, with pronunciation in brackets

hello
hola (oh-la) / hola (oh-la)

goodbye
adios (ah-dee-yoss) / adéu (ah-DEY-yoo)

good morning
buenas dias (bwen-as dee-yas) / bon dia (bon DEE-ya)

good afternoon
buenas tardes (bwen-as tar-des) / bona tarda (boh-na tar-da)

goodnight
buenas noches (bwen-as noh-chess) / bona nit (boh-na neet)

please
por favor (por FAH-vor) / si us plau (syoos-plow)

thank you (very much)
(muchas) gracias (moo-chas gra-see-yas) / moltes gràcies (moll gra-syes)

More expressions in Spanish and Catalan

I don't speak Spanish / Catalan
no hablo castellano / catalàn
no parlo castellà / català

do you speak English?
¿habla inglés? /¿parla anglès?

I don't understand
no entiendo / no l'entenc

speak more slowly, please
hable más despacio, por favor
pot parlar més poc a poc, si us plau

excuse me (for attention)
oiga /escolti

I'm sorry
perdón/perdoni

OK
vale/molt bé

yes – sí
no – no

Asking directions in Spanish

do you know the way to…?
sabe cómo llegar a…/ para ir a…?

train – tren
ticket – un billete
single ticket – billete sencillo

return – ida y vuelta
next stop – la próxima parada
how much is it?
cuánto es?

Booking a room in Spanish

do you have a double/single for tonight/three days/one week?
tiene una habitación doble/para una persona para esta noche/ tres dias/una semana?

I/we have a reservation
tengo/ tenemos reserva
with/without bathroom/shower – con/sin/ baño/ducha
double bed – cama doble
twin beds – con dos camas
breakfast included – desayuno incluido

Numbers

1 – un/uno/una
2 – dos
3 – tres
4 – cuatro
5 – cinco
6 – seis
7 – siete
8 – ocho
9 – nueve
10 – diez
11 – once

12 – doce
13 – trece
14 – catorce
15 – quinze
16 – dieciséis
17 – diecisiete
18 – dieciocho
19 – diecinueve
20 – veinte
21 – veintiuno
22 – veintidos
25 – veinitcinco
30 – treinta
40 – cuarenta
50 – cincuenta
60 – sesenta
70 – setenta
80 – ochenta
90 – noventa
100 – cien
200 – doscientos
253 – doscientos cincuenta y tres
1000 – mil
2000 – dos mil
1,000,000 – un millión

Days and Dates

Monday – Lunes
Tuesday – Martes
Wednesday – Miércoles
Thursday – Jueves
Friday – Viernes
Saturday – Sábado
Sunday – Domingo

January – Enero
February – Febrero
March – Marzo
April – Abril
May – Mayo
June – Junio
July – Julio
August – Agosto
September – Septiembre

October – Octubre
November – Noviembre
December Diciembre

Meeting People

what's your name?
cómo se llama?

my name is…
me llamo…

where are you from?
de dónde eres?

I'm Australian/ Canadian/English/ Irish/from New Zealand/ from the USA
soy australiano/a/ canadiense/ inglés/esa irlandés/esa de Nueva Zelanda, estadounidense

NB – to some, American (americano/ a) applies to North, South and Central America.

would you like a drink?
quiere beber algo?

would you like to dance?
quieres bailar?

you're very handsome
– eres muy guapo/a

can I take you to dinner?
te gustaría cenar

conmigo?
here's my number
– este es mi número

I have a boyfriend/girlfriend /partner – tengo novio/novia/pareja

do you have a condom? tienes un condón?

come and visit me in…
ven a verme en…

you made my stay in Barcelona very special –
hiciste mi estancía en Barcelona muy especial

INDEX

INDEX

NOTEBOOK

out AROUND **CONTACT LIST**

Name _____

Address _____

_____

_____

Tel _____

Fax _____

email _____

Name _____

Address _____

_____

_____

Tel _____

Fax _____

email _____

Name _____

Address _____

_____

_____

Tel _____

Fax _____

email _____

Name _____

Address _____

_____

_____

Tel _____

Fax _____

email _____

Name _____

Address _____

_____

_____

Tel _____

Fax _____

email _____

Name _____

Address _____

_____

_____

Tel _____

Fax _____

email _____

MY TOP RESTAURANTS

Fill in details of your favourite restaurants below . . .
Tell us about them by logging on to **www.outaround.com**

Restaurant

Contact Details

Comments

Restaurant

Contact Details

Comments

Restaurant

Contact Details

Comments

My Top Restaurants

MY TOP BARS

Fill in details of your favourite bars below . . .
Tell us about them by logging on to **www.outaround.com**

My Top Bars

Bar

Contact Details

Comments

Bar

Contact Details

Comments

Bar

Contact Details

Comments

Fill in details of your favourite clubs below . . .
Tell us about them by logging on to **www.outaround.com**

Club

Contact Details

Comments

Club

Contact Details

Comments

Club

Contact Details

Comments

AMSTERDAM

BARCELONA & SITGES

BERLIN

MIAMI

NEW YORK

LONDON

PARIS

SAN FRANCISCO

Out
AROUND

**Look for the
Rainbow Spine!**

**Your Gay Guide
to the World!**

Thomas Cook
Publishing